Myshel is truly an anointed young woman, an
experience her ministry is life-changing. Her book
help you discover your identity in Christ and live fearle
for him.

CeCe Winans, Christian Recording Arti

Myshel's passion and drive for women fall nothing short of dynamic. Her commitment to see women rise up from the clutches of mental and societal strongholds is shown in her words, her music, and her multifaceted expressions. This devotional is a beautiful extension of the depth and reach to which she goes to make sure every woman is equipped with the proper tools to overcome obstacles, win fearlessly, and rise in power.

Juliette Ross, Upset the World, LLC

I'm thrilled about this amazing forty-day devotional that challenges and encourages God's people to embrace their true identity. It's thought-provoking and life-changing, designed to propel you into your next season as God calls you to rise up. When you know your identity, you understand both your destiny and authority in God's kingdom. Enjoy this fantastic devotional from Myshel Wilkins!

Pastor Clyde Lewis, Destiny Church International

Arise, Shine, & CONQUER

40 DAYS OF COURAGE
FOR WOMEN

Myshel Wilkins

BroadStreet
PUBLISHING

BroadStreet Publishing® Group, LLC
Savage, Minnesota, USA
BroadStreetPublishing.com

Arise, Shine, and Conquer: 40 Days of Courage for Women

9781424568840 (faux leather)
9781424568857 (ebook)

Cover and interior by Garborg Design Works | garborgdesign.com

Printed in China

25 26 27 28 29 5 4 3 2 1

To my wonderful husband, my precious sons,
and my parents and siblings.
Your unwavering support is the wind beneath my wings and truly God's gift to my life.

Contents

Foreword

In a world that pulls us in a hundred different directions, there lies a profound truth calling us to live with intention and purpose. For that reason, I'm profoundly honored to present *Arise, Shine, and Conquer*, a powerful devotional inviting you to embrace each morning with gratitude, expectancy, and unwavering faith.

My dear friend Myshel has poured her heart into these pages, offering insight, wisdom, and encouragement to help you confront and overcome doubt, fear, and the challenges of life by standing firm in the knowledge that you are loved, equipped, and called for a purpose.

This devotional is not just a collection of reflections; it is a sacred, forty-day journey designed to inspire you to shine your unique light. No doubt that as you embark on this journey, you will experience a revival in your heart and mind that will uplift your spirit and embolden you to arise, shine, and conquer as God says you can!

Many blessings,
Kim Crabill

Introduction

Welcome to *Arise, Shine, and Conquer*, a transformative journey tailored for believers seeking empowerment, victory, and a deeper understanding of their identity in Jesus Christ. Without understanding our God-given identity, we can claim no God-given authority. God wants us to live and enjoy the gift he makes available to every believer: the power to overcome.

Born and raised in Frankfort, Kentucky, I traveled extensively with my father to many churches of different denominations and cultural backgrounds. Even as a young girl, I sensed that while some churches challenged their congregation to utilize their faith and believe God could do the impossible, many just seemed to enjoy a comfortable, social-club-like environment with little depth. My curiosity drove me to begin my search to discover if the God of the Bible still moved in great power in the twenty-first century.

I had to decide if I wanted comfort or if I wanted my faith to increase. Was I hungry for the Lord himself or just the good feelings he brought me? What did I really want from God? What kind of life was I willing to live for him?

I took some time to ponder and reflect on what it

would look like to live a life totally surrendered. After talking to God and watching strong Christians around me, the decision was clear. For me, it was all or nothing.

My decision to go all in left me standing in awe of God's miraculous power, his sweet presence in the midst of storms, and the wonderful tools he gave me to use in each daily battle. All these gifts illuminated God's love for his people and taught me that he would not leave us alone in the fight. I learned not to avoid challenges but instead to invite God into them and watch him work out all things for my good.

This book springs from my fervent desire to help fellow believers transcend every challenge and radiate the brilliance of Christ's glory. I long to encourage others to step out of their comfort zones and experience God in the deepest parts of their being. I desire to see the body of Christ leave nothing on the table and instead fully utilize every benefit, blessing, and spiritual provision that Christ's resurrection has given us.

Drawing from Scripture and my own experiences of tribulation and triumph, *Arise, Shine, and Conquer* offers practical insights, joyful encouragement, and spiritual strategies to guide you to the confidence and authority that comes from living in God's presence. You are a conqueror, and you are destined for greatness in Christ. Christ wants to be displayed in us and through us. No matter how difficult our circumstances, he will work all things together for our good.

Since Christ made freedom attainable, we are meant to possess it. Put on his freedom and walk in the fullness Christ intended for your life. When you live in this freedom and power, others will notice. God can then use you to spread his saving gospel of peace and hope amid every challenge.

Enter into God's Word today to receive his deep revelation and great anointing so that you can overcome sin. Our faith beckons us to embrace an abundant life rooted in the victory that Christ has secured for us through his redeeming sacrifice. Our Lord is inviting us into a partnership with him, one that will be the adventure of our lifetime and lead to our ultimate reward in heaven. Let's not miss it! I welcome you to embark on this journey of discovery with bold and relentless faith as we arise, shine, and conquer together in the name of Jesus.

DAY 1

Learning to Arise, Shine, and Conquer

Arise, shine; for your light has come!
And the glory of the LORD is risen upon you.
ISAIAH 60:1 NKJV

Isaiah 60:1 is dear to my heart because it is a call to celebrate and experience victories, blessings, and breakthroughs from God. This verse urges us to recognize where God's glory shines brightest and how we can reflect his radiance to others. Yet I've recently pondered whether these words also beckon us to rise from despair and boldly stand in God's presence during adversity. Could it be that this verse encourages us to remain steadfast amid heartache, allowing the Lord to reveal himself to a watching world through our surrendered hearts?

In the intricate tapestry of our lives, interwoven with threads of challenges and triumphs, there is a constant call from God for believers to arise, shine, and conquer, whether from the mountaintops of victory or the valleys of hardship. We do not achieve our victory through our strength but through the mighty name of Jesus.

I remember when I got the phone call that my beloved uncle, Pastor George A. Odoi, had passed away. It was unexpected, and I was devastated because he was one of my favorite human beings on the planet. Weighed down by sadness and despair, I traveled to Ghana to celebrate his life.

In Ghana, instead of going to a church or funeral home for the viewing or wake, they bring the body to the house to be viewed one last time. That's when I learned a life-altering lesson on the power of rising and shining in the middle of even the darkest moments of life. The family came together and simply worshiped. With hurting hearts and exhausted bodies, they worshiped with all their strength for hours before my uncle's body arrived. After watching them worship for a moment, I joined in with glorious fervor. I could feel the presence of the Lord so strongly around me that it nearly took my breath away.

The glory of the Lord was undoubtedly upon us. Friends and distant family surrounded us, some watching, some joining in worship, and in that moment, we all witnessed the glorious light of God as my uncle's family displayed a unified trust in the Lord. In this moment, I learned the power of worship.

This experience deeply affected me, and I vowed to worship through every trouble and heartache. I watched my family worship with passionate thanksgiving unto the Lord. It did not make natural sense to worship like this, but as Christians, it was simply the only option in the face of this world's despair. I was awestruck by the intense anointing that flooded the room.

Satan's power is real. We live in a sinful and fallen world, and we will experience attacks from the devil. But remember the comfort in Psalm 23:4, which says, "Even though I walk through the darkest valley, I will fear no evil, for you are with me; your rod and your staff, they comfort me" (NIV). This verse acknowledges the reality of darkness, but it also declares the promise of divine companionship, guiding us through the shadows into the light beyond.

To shine is to reflect the brilliance of God's love, mercy, and grace. As we navigate life's journey, our shining becomes a testimony to our unwavering faith in our Lord Jesus Christ. Proverbs 4:18 beautifully captures this idea: "The path of the righteous is like the morning sun, shining ever brighter till the full light of day" (NIV). As we navigate life's journey, let us radiate faith that grows brighter with each step, dispelling the shadows of doubt and fear.

Our faith is not contingent on our circumstances but anchored in the unchanging character of God. His power and glory are the greatest. Through him, we can arise, shine, and conquer through the battles we will face in life.

Father, guide me to arise, shine, and conquer in every circumstance in the powerful name of Jesus. As I navigate life's seasons, may my faith shine ever brighter, my purpose grow clearer, and my victories echo with the triumphant name of Jesus. Amen.

Today I arise, for the glory of our Lord shines upon me!

DAY 2

Faith in Action

What good is it, my brothers and sisters,
if someone claims to have faith but has no deeds?
Can such faith save them?
JAMES 2:14 NIV

Along life's journey, we will receive invitations to go beyond our comfort zones and partner with God to see his unprecedented miracles, favor, and divine provision. Some will accept the invitations. But others may not, as stepping out in faith requires a willingness to embrace discomfort and vulnerability. It means relinquishing control of our plans and agendas, trusting instead in the wisdom and sovereignty of God. It requires us to walk by faith, not by sight. Definitely not for the faint of heart.

In today's verse, James urges us to move beyond the realm of mere words into a life marked by real action. While praying, reading God's Word, and fasting are indispensable tools in our spiritual arsenal, these disciplines are not all we must do to live an active faith. Rather, they are instruments that powerfully sharpen our spiritual discernment and attune us to God's desires. In our communion with him, he guides us and gives us the clarity and strength we need to follow the Holy Spirit, take strategic action, and leave an impact. This is how he readies us to engage with the world.

On the flip side, when we don't listen to God and read his Word, we may do things that seem good and noble but that God has not actually assigned us to do. We tie our identities or spiritual values to the idea that we must always be working for God rather than working to know who God is. Thus, the battle between a good idea and a God idea begins. We must pray for discernment to know the difference and the wisdom to find our identity in Christ alone.

Hebrews 11:1 encapsulates the essence of faith, describing it as the "confidence in what we hope for and the assurance about what we do not see" (NIV). In the book of Esther, Queen Esther prayed, fasted, and risked her life in faith. In the narrative of the paralyzed man lowered through the roof to reach Jesus (Mark 2:1–12), we read another powerful display of faith in action. The paralyzed man's friends didn't stop at praying or discussing; they took decisive steps that ended in a miracle.

Faith-filled action is hardly ever comfortable. There

is always an earthly cost. Yet when the Holy Spirit is leading, your actions will bear much fruit. Like God called Queen Esther and the paralyzed man's friends, he calls us to be catalysts of change, breaking through barriers and obstacles in our pursuit of God's transformative power. Our deeds should display an outpouring of our unwavering confidence in the promises of God. Let us embrace a faith that compels us into action and pushes us out of our comfort zone.

Similarly, our faith is most potent when it finds expression in love-driven actions that influence the lives of those around us. We must remember that love is not just a noun; it's a verb. You can find this in the apostle John's exhortation in 1 John 3:18: "Dear children, let us not love with words or speech but with actions and in truth" (NIV). Prayer and fasting fuel our hearts with divine love, propelling us to manifest that love in substantial, transformative actions. As we engage in acts of kindness, compassion, and justice, we become conduits of God's divine love in a broken world.

Father, in the name of Jesus, I ask that you help me to embrace a faith that transcends the boundaries of words and abstentions, propelling me into a life of dynamic, Holy Spirit-led action. May my faith be a force that moves mountains, transforms lives, and reflects the love of Christ through my intentional and impactful deeds. Amen.

Faith, when coupled with action, becomes a glorious testimony to the power of a life that impacts others in the name of Christ.

DAY 3

Building Beyond Walls

"Come, let us rebuild the wall of Jerusalem, and we will no longer be in disgrace."
NEHEMIAH 2:17 NIV

Nehemiah's story is one of my favorites in the Bible. He stands as a timeless example of visionary leadership and unwavering faith. I have used Nehemiah's story to train ministry leaders and to teach my young son how to handle bullies on the playground. Through God's power, Nehemiah stayed focused on the truth and the task at hand, despite facing countless false accusations, constant mocking, and terrifying threats. Let's take a closer look at his amazing story.

Nehemiah, a cupbearer to the king, received a message from God to rebuild the walls of Jerusalem and to restore honor and dignity to the people of Israel. This divine assignment became the cornerstone of his leadership. He took on this huge project not for recognition but because the Lord led him.

Nehemiah 1:4 records Nehemiah's initial response to the news of Jerusalem's broken walls: "I sat down and wept. For some days I mourned and fasted and prayed before the God of heaven." Nehemiah combined strategic planning, fervent prayer, and a compassionate heart before taking any action. He sought God's guidance through consistent conversations with him, allowing the Lord to turn his desires to only what God wanted.

The most impressive part about this story is that Nehemiah's leadership did not end with the completion of the walls. He established systems of governance that ensured the sustainability of the rebuilt city. In Nehemiah 7:2, he appointed trustworthy leaders to oversee the city, leaving a legacy of effective leadership. Nehemiah's commitment to building beyond his immediate project emphasizes the importance of considering the futures of the people we lead. This practice deeply resonates with me when it comes to missions.

I have traveled and served with my missionary father in several countries since I was young. Too often, I'd see missionaries do good work in the present but forget about the future of the people they were serving. Some teams would work in an area for several months, but once they left, the people returned to their previous state of poverty and hopelessness.

This outcome frustrated me. Our efforts to help

people must result in a sustainable plan for long-term change and empowerment. Healthy mission work involves providing the means for long-term improvements such as vocational training, schools, farming, nutritional education, and access to medical assistance. But without the Lord's guidance, no missionary can ever establish a system that creates lasting change and self-sufficiency.

I've witnessed great movements rise and fall because of the stress and striving that comes from implementing an idea, even a good idea, without guidance from the Lord. It may help people at first, but it soon becomes a source of disappointment if the leaders don't turn to the Lord for discernment and direction. A leader risks devastating their relationships and family when they choose to take on a task without the blessing of God.

With the projects we take on, both great and small, we have to ask ourselves: Is this a good idea or a God idea? What compels us to do the things we do, and are we following the leading of the Holy Spirit?

Let us grasp the profound truth that strategic leadership is born in the secret place of prayer, where God saturates our hearts in passion and compels us to see his vision fulfilled. Through prayer, he gives us what we need and moves the hearts of others. Remember, prayer is not preparation for the battle—it is the battle. Strategic plans gain potency when we saturate them in prayer because God is in control of the plan instead of us.

We must invest in other people and create enduring structures to ensure the lasting success of our efforts in God's ministry. May we place our time, energy and hearts into the plans and desires that come from the Lord.

Father, in the name of Jesus, I pray that I will glean transformative insights from Nehemiah's leadership journey. May I, like Nehemiah, build with purpose, lead with prayerful wisdom, confront opposition with unwavering faith, and foster unity among those you would have me lead. Amen.

I am inspired to build with vision, integrity, and an enduring commitment to God's life-changing purposes.

DAY 4

Hidden Treasure in the Dark

Dear friends, do not be surprised at the fiery ordeal that has come on you to test you, as though something strange were happening to you.
1 PETER 4:12 NIV

After weeks of celebrating the news that we were having a baby and preparing to receive this wonderful gift, we went back to the doctor for a routine check-up only to hear them say that they could no longer detect the heartbeat of our little one. We were devastated. Grief and blame bombarded my mind. *How could this happen to me? I don't deserve this. Why would God allow this to happen? I'm a good person!*

In our faith journey, we often encounter trials that challenge our convictions, leaving us grappling with the notion of *I've heard this happen to others, but why did this happen to me?* It is a common temptation to believe that our commitment to serving God should shield us from life's devastations. Entitlement creeps in, whispering that our faithfulness should exempt us from hardships. Even if we would never say it aloud, it's so easy to let these thoughts nestle deep within our hearts without even realizing it.

Our trials are not indicators of God's disfavor but opportunities for his grace to abound. In 1 Peter 4:12–13, we find solace:

> Dear friends, do not be surprised at the fiery ordeal that has come on you to test you, as though something strange were happening to you. But rejoice inasmuch as you participate in the sufferings of Christ, so that you may be overjoyed when his glory is revealed. (NIV)

I've had a total of eight miscarriages and can testify that although it wasn't easy, I found sweet treasures of God's protection, provision, and healing in the most difficult and dark times of my life. Treasures that transformed my life for the better. Entitlement would have destroyed my chance to find the beauty God had placed in my life, even in the midst of these difficult situations.

Entitlement stems from a misplaced sense of self-importance. Job, a biblical figure known for his trials, provides a profound lesson in humility. Despite his righteousness, Job faced immense suffering. In Job 42:2–3, he humbly acknowledges,

> I know that you can do all things; no purpose of yours can be thwarted. You asked, "Who is this that obscures my plans without knowledge?"
> Surely I spoke of things I did not understand, things too wonderful for me to know. (NIV)

I can agree with Job. I was determined not to allow this unanswered why become a wall between me and the Lord. As Job said in Job 42:5, "My ears had heard of you but now my eyes have seen you" (NIV). God was giving me the opportunity to see him in ways I'd never experienced when my life was easy. I knew that God loved me and that he would carry me through this time with his indescribable grace. It was a beautiful experience that fortified my love and trust in him. Entitlement crumbles in the face of acknowledging God's sovereignty over our lives.

As you face trials, let humility replace entitlement as you recognize that your understanding is finite while God's wisdom is boundless. When entitlement whispers that you deserve an easy path, echo Habakkuk's resolve to find joy in God regardless of external conditions (Habakkuk 3:17–19). Your faith will grow stronger when it rests not on entitlement but on the unchanging character of our Savior.

In 1 Thessalonians 5:18, we are urged to "give thanks in all circumstances; for this is God's will for you in Christ Jesus" (NIV). I cannot emphasize enough how powerful gratitude is in transforming our perspectives. Look for the blessings that are ever present within each trial. You will marvel at how many sweet treasures you will find within moments of pain and grief, for you are not alone. God is with you. Intentionally cultivate a heart of gratitude that will redirect your focus and allow you to acknowledge the countless blessings God bestows on you even during your trials.

Heavenly Father, I pray that you will help me to navigate the delicate terrain of trials with faith, humility, and gratitude. I can find joy in noticing that in this valley, I will get to know you in ways I couldn't on a mountaintop, and for this, I will forever give you praise. Amen.

May I find the sweet treasure of knowing him more deeply in my darkest seasons.

DAY 5

Embracing Our God-Given Identity

I praise you because I am
fearfully and wonderfully made.
PSALM 139:14 NIV

The question of identity stands as a pivotal theme in today's world. The younger generations face countless voices from all directions, each attempting to define their identity. But what is our God-given identity, and how do we find it?

Scripture serves as the foundational mirror, reflecting our true identity. Today's verse shows us that our identity is fearfully, wonderfully, and carefully crafted by a very intentional Creator who loves us and has a beautiful reason for calling us into existence. We must understand that our identity is not rooted in the world's ever-changing opinions, achievements, or failures but in the unchanging character of our heavenly Father.

In order to live in our true identity, we must believe God's declaration over our lives. In Isaiah 43:1, God proclaims, "Fear not, for I have redeemed you; I have called you by your name; you are Mine" (NKJV). You see, God's declaration over us supersedes any other label the world may place upon us. Everything God says is truth. You are his, and he has redeemed you.

Unfortunately, the reality is that this world is filled with deception that presents itself as glorious truth but will only set us on a path that leads to destruction. We must ask God to help us shut out the noise of the world. Only then can we listen for his voice and hear who he says we truly are, for only in God will we find our true selves.

Our identity is not subject to change or compromise; it is firmly established in the redemptive work of Christ. The world bombards us with lies about our worth, purpose, and capabilities, yet 2 Corinthians 10:5 urges us to "take captive every thought to make it obedient to Christ" (NIV). This involves discerning the lies, replacing them with the truth of God's Word, and living them out daily.

As you navigate life's challenges, know that you are redeemed, called, loved, and fully accepted by God. When the Enemy whispers doubt, reminding you of past mistakes or inadequacies, counter those lies with the truth that you are fearfully and wonderfully made for an important purpose. Living in our God-given identities requires a vigilant heart that confronts falsehood with the unstoppable truth of God's eternal declarations over us.

To put it simply, it is impossible to walk in our true identity if we do not fully believe who God says we are in him. When we align our thoughts and beliefs with God's truth, our actions will naturally follow suit.

Philippians 2:5 instructs us to "have the same mindset as Christ Jesus" (NIV). As we strive to adopt the mind of Christ, we must align our thoughts with God's perspective on our identity.

How do we do this? It's simple—read the love letters he left for you and absorb them into your spirit and soul. These letters are the Word of God. With daily reading, these words can transform your thinking and, ultimately, your entire life. Let us intentionally cultivate the mind of Christ, embracing the truth that we are beloved, chosen, and called according to his purpose.

James 1:22 challenges us to be doers of the Word, not hearers only. When it comes to identity, this verse urges us to translate our knowledge into lived-out reality. As we grasp the truth of who God says we are, let our actions reflect the authenticity of our identity in Christ. Let us not say we are fearfully and wonderfully made and then stand in the mirror at home and tear ourselves down. We must deeply believe God's words.

Our true identity is not a passive reality but a transformative force that influences our relationships, decisions, and responses to life's challenges. To live this out, we must intentionally align ourselves with God's Word in every aspect of our lives.

Father, in the name of Jesus, I pray that I will live in my God-given identity. As I confront lies, adopt the mind of Christ, and walk in confidence, I pray that my life will reflect the authenticity that you desire I display to a world still searching for purpose. Amen.

Living in my true identity is not a passive acknowledgment but an active, transformative journey that will impact my legacy and the world around me.

DAY 6

Breaking the Chains of Fear

God has not given us a spirit of fear,
but of power and of love and of a sound mind.
2 TIMOTHY 1:7 NKJV

In the realm of spiritual warfare, one of the most insidious weapons the Enemy employs is the spirit of fear. Today, we will unveil the tactics of the spirit of fear and discover how it seeks to undermine and distort the purpose of believers in Christ.

Scripture warns us that "we do not wrestle against flesh and blood" but against spiritual forces (Ephesians 6:12 ESV). The spirit of fear is not a fleeting emotion but a strategic tool Satan uses to cripple, paralyze, and distort the purpose that God has ordained for his children. We must understand the nature of this tool to overcome its influence. At the core of Satan's strategy is the corruption of God's promises. For example, since God promised that he will never leave nor forsake us, Satan will inject fear into your heart, telling you that you are all alone, forsaken, an unloved orphan.

God says in Malachi 3:10:

> Bring ye all the tithes into the storehouse, that there may be meat in mine house, and prove me now herewith, saith the Lord of hosts, if I will not open you the windows of heaven, and pour you out a blessing, that there shall not be room enough to receive it. (KJV)

Fear says you won't have enough for yourself if you do this. Fear wants to convince you that God is a liar and cannot be trusted. We can either choose to believe this lie or God's promises of adoption and love.

The original word in the Greek language for the phrase "sound mind" in today's verse is *sóphronismos*. This word means "self-control" or "moderation."[1] Second Timothy 1:7 instructs us not to act in fear or be irrationally minded but to act within God's will and be reasonable in our thoughts and ways. God's thoughts are reasonable and beautiful, whereas thoughts that sprout from fear are always unreasonable.

The spirit of fear also turns our focus inward, overwhelming us with worry about what people will

---

1 Strong, *Strong's Expanded Exhaustive Concordance of the Bible*, G4995.

think about us. When I started working in the Christian music industry, I was overwhelmed with doubt about my own self-worth. I constantly compared myself—my looks, my talent, my personality—to others. Rather than building my life on the solid rock of Christ's view of me, I built on the shifting sand of the world's expectations.

The truth was that I believed I was not good enough. No matter what I did, the spirit of perfectionism nearly suffocated me. I knew that if I continued in this belief, it would derail me from fulfilling my purpose. I'd find myself worn out and worn down from the constant hamster wheel of life, and that would steal my joy and witness. I had to get off the wheel, deal with the roots of my belief system, call out the lies, ask God for deliverance, and accept the gift of freedom he offered.

Philippians 4:6–7 offers a strategy:

> Be anxious for nothing, but in everything by prayer and supplication, with thanksgiving, let your requests be made known to God; and the peace of God, which surpasses all understanding, will guard your hearts and minds through Christ Jesus. (NKJV)

Sometimes a scarcity mindset will tell us we don't have enough of what we need. In Matthew 6:26, Jesus reminds us, "Look at the birds of the air; they do not sow or reap or store away in barns, and yet your heavenly Father feeds them. Are you not much more valuable than they?" (NIV). Satan uses fear to convince believers that God's provision is insufficient or unreliable. And fear doesn't just affect our spirits and emotions; it also creates stress that affects our physical health.

The great news is that fear loses its grip when we acknowledge God as our ultimate provider and sustainer. Living in the assurance of God's provision and promise allows believers to pursue their purpose confidently and boldly. Why should I live like a slave when I am an heir to the King of kings? I am royalty, and he sacrificed himself for my inheritance. I don't want to leave a single gift on the table. I receive it all in the powerful name of Jesus! If freedom is mine, then, indeed, I shall have it.

Heavenly Father, I thank you for unveiling Satan's tool of fear and fortifying my heart in your promises. I refuse the spirit of fear that works to distort your promises, paralyze me with anxiety, and create doubt in your goodness. Today, I choose to believe you, Lord. Amen.

Today I will confidently protect the sound mind that God has graciously given me by believing every word he says.

DAY 7

Overcoming Temptation

Each one is tempted when he is drawn away by his own desires and enticed. Then, when desire has conceived, it gives birth to sin; and sin, when it is full-grown, brings forth death.

JAMES 1:14–15 NKJV

Everyone has been tempted to sin. Scripture warns us about the allure of temptation, recognizing its potential to entice and ensnare. Temptation is not merely a fleeting inclination but also a strategic ploy to lead believers away from God's path. Understanding the nature of temptation is crucial in fortifying ourselves against its destructive impact on our lives. Left unchecked, it will undermine the spiritual vitality of believers. It starts as a subtle tug, enticing individuals away from the vibrancy of their relationship with God. This is why we should guard our spiritual fervor, recognizing that the Enemy seeks to dim the light of our faith.

In Revelation 3:15–16, Jesus warns against spiritual lukewarmness:

> I know your deeds, that you are neither cold nor hot. I wish you were either one or the other! So, because you are lukewarm—neither hot nor cold—I am about to spit you out of my mouth. (NIV)

Temptation, when we entertain it, contributes to this lukewarm state, threatening the depth and warmth of our connection with God and ensnaring believers in an ongoing cycle of sin that leads to death. It does so subtly. The longer we spend near temptation, the harder it will be to resist. When you sense temptation stirring, run in the other direction.

Temptation always offers an unfair exchange. You get something that temporarily appeases your flesh, and the Enemy takes something that devastates your spirit. Unfortunately, this is what happened in the garden of Eden. Nothing is worth desecrating our integrity and tarnishing our witness. God has given believers a Christ-centered influence to impact our families, communities, and beyond.

When we give in to temptation, we lose some of this influence over others. Proverbs 6:27–28 cautions, "Can a man scoop fire into his lap without his clothes being burned? Can a man walk on hot coals without his feet being scorched?" (NIV). From tempting you to watch pornography to urging you to cheat on your taxes, the Enemy doesn't play fair and works to blind us from the reality that our lives are a living testimony to the transformative power of Christ. Yielding to temptation diminishes this testimony and casts a shadow on the authenticity of our faith. We may even accidentally cause unbelievers we know to doubt the sustaining power of God.

The beauty in all of this is that God's grace and intense love are illuminated in these tough moments. The Father's heart is reflected in the parable of the prodigal son. When we fall into temptation, we must simply turn and ask for forgiveness, and he is so eager to receive us again.

Additionally, Hebrews 4:15 says,

> We do not have a High Priest who is unable to sympathize and understand our weaknesses and temptations, but One who has been tempted [knowing exactly how it feels to be human] in every respect as we are, yet without [committing any] sin. (AMP)

Jesus faced the same struggles we face today. When you are at your lowest moments, turn to him for the strength to stay free from sin and for the hope that heaven is in your future.

One of my favorite verses is Hebrews 12:1. It says, "Since we are surrounded by such a great cloud of witnesses, let us throw off everything that hinders and the sin that so easily entangles. And let us run with perseverance the race marked out for us" (NIV).

I am a visual person, so I imagine loved ones who have transitioned to heaven cheering me on, shouting, "Keep going, Myshel; stay free and focused on Jesus. You can do it!"

And there is even more good news. The Bible also shows us that Jesus speaks to the Father on our behalf. Romans 8:34 says that Jesus "is at the right hand of God and is also interceding for us" (NIV). In 1 John 2:1, we read that Jesus is our "advocate with the Father" (NIV). Temptations will come, but the temptations themselves are not sinful. We must not succumb to them, for that is when we open our lives to evils that God does not want for us.

But thanks be to God that with his guidance, we can overcome all the temptations of this world so we can run with perseverance the race he has marked out for us.

Father, I see how temptation undermines spiritual vitality and robs believers of your best. Help me to discern your path and make choices that bring peace and life. With you, I shall rise above the enticements of temptation, safeguarding my heart to experience the fullness of the abundant life Christ offers. Amen.

My eyes are open, and my heart is fixed on choosing the Lord's way every day of my life.

DAY 8

Your God-Given Authority

"Behold, I give you the authority to trample on serpents and scorpions, and over all the power of the enemy, and nothing shall by any means hurt you."
LUKE 10:19 NKJV

I used to attend a church that didn't believe God still performed miracles today. Believers were encouraged to look only to the past for God's power rather than the present. But when I visited the mission field, I saw missionaries, filled with God's power and authority, perform miracles right in front of me! God is not dead, and neither is his power. Just like the disciples, we are entrusted with God's authority and called to use it wisely.

In Matthew 16:19, Jesus was talking to Peter and said, "I will give you the keys of the kingdom of heaven; whatever you bind on earth will be bound in heaven, and whatever you loose on earth will be loosed in heaven" (NIV). This verse is crucial to understanding authority in Christ. In Jewish culture, *bind* and *loose* were legal terms that meant to declare something forbidden or allowed. The disciples were given authority and were to fulfill God's plan with it, and so are we today.

Jesus reaffirmed this authority in the Great Commission, found in Matthew 28:18–19: "All authority in heaven and on earth has been given to me. Therefore go and make disciples of all nations" (NIV).

In Acts 4:7, after a man was healed, the religious authorities asked Peter and John, "By what power or what name did you do this?" (NIV). In other words, "By what authority were you able to do this?" In verse 10, Peter answered,

> Let me clearly state to all of you and to all the people of Israel that he was healed by the powerful name of Jesus Christ the Nazarene, the man you crucified but whom God raised from the dead. (NLT)

Peter took no credit for the miracle but boldly announced to all the people of Israel that the power of Jesus accomplished this miracle.

It is not by our might nor our power but by the Spirit of the living God that we exercise his authority on the earth. We should be careful to remember that we can't use this authority to change God's mind or do whatever we want. Rather when a believer binds and looses something under God's authority, they do so out of God's word. They use the name that is above every name, the one with all authority, Jesus the Anointed One. God gives us our authority for no other purpose but to display his glory and power on the earth.

We should not view understanding and walking in this authority as an option but as a vital aspect of the Christian journey and the foundation for a victorious and purposeful life. There are consequences to underestimating our God-given authority. When believers fail to walk in their authority, they risk falling prey to the Enemy's schemes. First Peter 5:8 warns, "Be alert and of sober mind. Your enemy the devil prowls around like a roaring lion looking for someone to devour" (NIV).

The Enemy exploits believers' vulnerabilities and capitalizes on their ignorance of the spiritual weapons available to them. If soldiers are unfamiliar with their weapons or lack proper combat training, they cannot expect to advance and be victorious in battle. A soldier must dress the part, understand the objective, and master their weapons. Much like soldiers have to overcome enemies in battle, it is up to us to successfully overcome the Enemy of our lives.

Remember God has given us the authority to trample on snakes and scorpions and to overcome all the power of the Enemy. Just as Jesus says in Matthew 28, we are to boldly advance the kingdom through the authority Christ has given us. When believers shrink back from their God-given authority, they diminish their impact on the kingdom. Jesus said to go! And as we go, the power of his authority will accompany us.

Heavenly Father, as I walk in my God-given authority, unlock in me your transformative power that ushers in victory, purpose, and abundant living in Jesus' name. Thank you, Lord, for giving me spiritual weapons that push back the darkness and reveal your glorious kingdom here on earth. Amen.

Jesus has given me the authority to trample on snakes and scorpions and to overcome all the power of the Enemy.

DAY 9

The Necessity of a Prayer Life

We do not wrestle against flesh and blood, but against principalities, against powers, against the rulers of the darkness of this age, against spiritual hosts of wickedness in the heavenly places.
EPHESIANS 6:12 NKJV

Life gets so busy, doesn't it? I have had days that start with an early flight, and once I hit the ground, I'm running all day until late in the evening, and by then I'm exhausted. The moment my head hits the pillow, I think, *Oh Lord, I didn't get to spend my quiet time with you.* I always whisper prayers throughout the day, but it isn't the same as when I quiet all the noise and intentionally focus on time with my Lord.

I'm sure you can relate to this. You face so many

demands on your time, each bringing new difficulties, and soon you're jumping from task to task, guilty that you haven't spent time with God. However, there's no need to be so hard on yourself. The good news is that the Lord understands and is ready to meet with us wherever we make time to do so. But to maintain a thriving relationship with God, we do need to spend quality time with him.

A thriving prayer life cultivates intimacy with God, leading to a genuine friendship and deepening our communion with him. Through prayer, the Holy Spirit transforms us into the likeness of Christ. Second Corinthians 3:18 says, "We all, with unveiled face, beholding as in a mirror the glory of the Lord, are being transformed into the same image from glory to glory, just as by the Spirit of the Lord" (NKJV). When I spend time with the Lord, he changes me, growing me and maturing me so I can look more and more like him.

As I read the Word of God, I always pray and ask the Holy Spirit to open Scripture so that I can see his glory. Prayer opens the door to a deeper understanding of Scripture and a greater sensitivity to the Spirit's leading through the chapters and verses of the Word of God. It also strengthens your spirit, especially in times of uncertainty and adversity.

Prayer keeps me steady, sober-minded, and sensitive to the Lord. Matthew 11:28–30 says,

> Come to me, all you who are weary and burdened, and I will give you rest. Take my yoke upon you and learn from me, for I am gentle and humble in heart, and you will find rest for your souls. For my yoke is easy and my burden is light. (NIV)

I can't tell you how grateful I am that I can go and just lay out in his presence and say, Lord, I've come for an exchange. Here, you take this super heavy burden that is wearing me out, and I'll take your easy and light burden. I don't have to smoke, drink, or drug the burdens of my heart away; I can just give them to the Lord. He will help me navigate through all the weights in my life.

The benefits of cultivating a healthy prayer life are limitless. James 5:16 teaches that "the prayer of a righteous person is powerful and effective" (NIV), capable of bringing about healing and restoration. I've heard testimony after testimony of miracles and breakthroughs that occurred thanks to the power of prayer. I've witnessed marriages restored, the sick healed, and impossible situations turned completely around due to the glory of God. My faith skyrockets every time I watch the power of prayer work in my life and the lives of others.

It can happen anywhere—on a flight, in the middle of the night while you rock your baby back to sleep, in the parking lot before going into the store, on your lunch break, or while taking a walk. Whenever you find time to spend with the Lord, take advantage of it. He loves you and is eager to spend time with you. He looks forward to sharing his heart with you as well as hearing you speak to him.

Father, in the name of Jesus, I am grateful that all I need to do is spend time with you, and I will receive the blessings of your royal inheritance. You transform me as I experience you in ways that bring me so much peace and joy. I love you, Lord, with all my heart. Amen.

Oh, what needless pain I bear, all because I do not carry everything to God in prayer.

DAY 10

The Transforming Power of Forgiveness

See to it that no one falls short of the grace of God and that no bitter root grows up to cause trouble and defile many.

HEBREWS 12:15 NIV

I remember one Sunday when God brought to my attention a family member whom I had refused to forgive. I had been holding on to resentment, feeling justified and powerful in keeping them hostage in my heart. However, I didn't realize that my refusal to forgive was actually hurting me. When God showed me during the church service how this grudge was attacking my spirit, I went to the altar, fell on my knees, and released my burden.

The next thing that happened still gives me chill

bumps. The glory of the Lord completely overwhelmed me. I couldn't move or talk for nearly thirty minutes after I surrendered. I felt God's great pleasure, and it changed me forever.

Forgiveness is essential for believers, for the foundation of our salvation is the fact that we have been forgiven for our sins. Even though it may not be easy, we must be willing to extend the same grace to others when we need to. Forgiveness is a powerful force that brings transformation not only to the person who is forgiven but also to the forgiver. It leads to restoration and profound freedom.

The truth is, harboring unforgiveness is like nurturing a bitter root within the soul, a root that can spread like a deadly virus and contaminate every aspect of your life. Unforgiveness weighs heavy on the heart, hindering spiritual growth and imprisoning the soul in a cycle of bitterness. It becomes the ball and chain attached to our heart, preventing forward movement in our journey with Christ.

Matthew 6:14–15 says, "If you forgive other people when they sin against you, your heavenly Father will also forgive you. But if you do not forgive others their sins, your Father will not forgive your sins" (NIV). This means that forgiveness is an act of obedience. Breaking chains of resentment requires a conscious decision to forgive, not based on the offender's actions but on obedience to God's command.

Ephesians 4:32 provides a foundational principle for forgiveness: "Be kind and compassionate to one another, forgiving each other, just as in Christ God forgave you" (NIV). Christ's forgiveness was not contingent on the worthiness of those he forgave but on the depth of his love and the extent of God's grace. Thanks to the Holy Spirit, we, too, can emulate Christ's forgiveness—a forgiveness rooted in love and driven by compassion.

Colossians 3:13 encourages believers to "bear with each other and forgive one another if any of you has a grievance against someone. Forgive as the Lord forgave you" (NIV). When we extend forgiveness, we release the burden of resentment and bitterness. In forgiving as the Lord forgave, our hearts become free to experience the fullness of God's love and grace. Forgiveness is the key that unlocks the gates of our heart, allowing healing to flow.

And in many cases, forgiveness opens the door to healing and restoration in both your soul and your physical body. Studies have found that the act of forgiveness can reap huge rewards for your health, lowering the risk of heart attack; improving cholesterol levels; and improving sleep, blood pressure, anxiety levels, depression, and stress.[2]

Through forgiveness, we yield to God's desire for us and allow him to release a healing that will go far

2 "Forgiveness: Your Health Depends on It," Johns Hopkins Medicine, https://www.hopkinsmedicine.org.

beyond what we could ever imagine, from today's sins to generational scars your family has struggled with longer than you can remember. My sister, my brother, choose to forgive. Ask the Holy Spirit to highlight anyone you may need to extend forgiveness to. Don't put it off another day.

Father, in the name of Jesus, I thank you for the opportunity to embrace the transformative power of forgiveness. I recognize the weight of unforgiveness, and I desire to emulate you. As you forgave me, so, too, will I choose to forgive others. I rejoice that you will liberate my heart. Amen.

May the liberating power of forgiveness bless my spirit, soul, and body.

DAY 11

Do I Resent God's Goodness?

"I say to you, love your enemies, bless those who curse you, do good to those who hate you, and pray for those who spitefully use you and persecute you."
MATTHEW 5:44 NKJV

Can I be honest? Today's devotion is a tough one. It's hard to understand why God would offer forgiveness to those who have deeply wronged us. But we must always remember that we serve a God who is radical in his grace and mercy, who often upends what we perceive as fairness. We must be willing to surrender our hearts to his ways, regardless of the cost, at every moment of our lives. This is the God we worship, and this is his path.

Through the lens of Scripture, we will navigate the complexities of accepting God's redemption under the most challenging circumstances. I'm certain that Christ was aware that his listeners did not welcome the command in today's verse. The radical nature of this command challenges us to put God's desires above our own in everything, even extending love and forgiveness to those who have wronged us deeply.

When God forgives those who have offended us, he compels us to confront our emotions and unearth our resentment. In moments of anger, we must face our feelings honestly and acknowledge that we are struggling to understand God's unfathomable grace.

The mysterious nature of God's love is displayed in Isaiah 55:9, which reminds us, "As the heavens are higher than the earth, so are my ways higher than your ways and my thoughts than your thoughts" (NIV). We don't need to understand God's ways; we just need to trust him. The nature of God's love and his sovereign wisdom will always surpass human understanding. Despite our discomfort or reservations, God's ways are higher, and his forgiveness extends to all who genuinely seek it.

Romans 12:19 says, "Do not take revenge, my dear friends, but leave room for God's wrath, for it is written: 'It is mine to avenge; I will repay,' says the Lord" (NIV). We can walk away from this verse thinking, *Yes! Go get them, God!* But what if your enemies ask forgiveness and God grants their prayer to be washed clean instead? We have no problem welcoming this forgiveness for ourselves, but somehow we find it difficult to extend that same forgiveness to those who have wronged us.

This difficulty reminds me of Jonah. God forgave Jonah for running away from him, but then Jonah was irritated with the Lord for extending mercy and grace to the Ninevites. Jonah 4:1–4 says,

> To Jonah this seemed very wrong, and he became angry. He prayed to the Lord, "Isn't this what I said, Lord, when I was still at home? That is what I tried to forestall by fleeing to Tarshish. I knew that you are a gracious and compassionate God, slow to anger and abounding in love, a God who relents from sending calamity. Now, Lord, take away my life, for it is better for me to die than to live." But the Lord replied, "Is it right for you to be angry?" (NIV)

I love the question God asks Jonah: "Is it right for you to be angry?" Jonah had forgotten that God had forgiven him of his mistakes, and he was angry that God was forgiving people whom Jonah wanted God to judge instead. Anger at wrongdoers is natural, but who are we to decide whom God forgives? The question is not, "Is it fair?" Instead, ask, "Was the mercy extended to us fair?" The answer will always be no; grace and mercy are not fair. That's what makes them so amazingly humbling. God's choice not to punish us reveals his goodness.

God calls us to see the world from his supernatural

perspective. If we don't, we cannot pray for our enemies or share the gospel in the darkest of places. Remember that he longs to use us to reach every corner of the world. Let us all be grateful for his goodness, grace, and extravagant mercy.

Father, I accept the beauty of your love, grace, and restorative power toward all your children. I release the burden of unforgiveness and choose to forgive. Lord, help me to pray for my enemies. Give me the desire to see them free and whole, just as you desire for all those you love. Amen.

If it were not for forgiveness, I would be utterly lost in my sin. I praise God for his amazing grace toward me.

DAY 12

Overcoming Comparison

They, measuring themselves by themselves, and comparing themselves among themselves, are not wise.
2 CORINTHIANS 10:12 NKJV

Comparison will steal the joy that comes with living in God's love. It is a subtle but destructive trap that hinders our spiritual growth, and it is impossible to survive on our own. When we compare ourselves to the people around us, we will begin to believe false narratives. We will see ourselves not as God sees us but instead as we think other people see us. This only leads to feelings of inadequacy or superiority, all built on the rotten fruits of envy, pride, ingratitude, and competition. We must recognize the dangers of comparison and seek wisdom from God to align our perspective with his truth.

First Samuel 16:7 reminds believers, "The LORD does not look at the things people look at. People look at the outward appearance, but the LORD looks at the heart" (NIV). The earthly standards of success, beauty, and achievement are limited and superficial. To build your identity on such shifting ground will leave you unstable. To lead a life based on God's truth, we must prioritize his eternal perspective over worldly standards. God values our heart—our character, intentions, and love—over anything else. Philippians 4:11–13 expresses the secret to contentment:

> I am not saying this because I am in need, for I have learned to be content whatever the circumstances. I know what it is to be in need, and I know what it is to have plenty. I have learned the secret of being content in any and every situation, whether well fed or hungry, whether living in plenty or in want. I can do all this through him who gives me strength. (NIV)

May we all cultivate a heart of contentment that springs from a rich and mature relationship with Christ. God's love is the source of strength, joy, fulfillment, and gratitude. It provides inner peace that overshadows the empty pursuits of comparison. You are intentionally unique, and the Lord leads your purpose and direction in life. We all have different callings for our lives, but we are united by one goal: to reflect his glory and beauty in the world. Our time here is short, so let's focus on fulfilling our God-given purpose rather than secretly competing against each other and comparing our ministries, purposes, and lifestyles.

Zephaniah 3:17 beautifully captures God's affirmation and love:

> The LORD your God is with you, the Mighty Warrior who saves. He will take great delight in you; in his love he will no longer rebuke you, but will rejoice over you with singing. (NIV)

God takes delight in you! He wants the best for you, and that doesn't include competing against other believers. Such competition only wastes time and emotion we could be using to do God's work here on earth. When we anchor our worth in God's affirmation, it becomes a powerful shield against the arrows of comparison. God rejoices in you! He created you, which means you are enough just the way you are.

First Thessalonians 5:18 instructs believers to "give thanks in all circumstances; for this is God's will for you in Christ Jesus" (NIV). Let's commit to focusing on gratitude, gratitude when we see others blessed, gratitude when we see our brothers and sisters experience the favor of God. May we thank God and celebrate others, never believing that it takes something away from us. May our hearts be joyful and grateful for what we have, where we are, and what God is doing for others. Let's praise God for what he has given us.

If we find ourselves tangled in the web of comparison that leaves us jealous or ungrateful, it's time to repent to the Lord and receive his perspective. I love the old hymn that says, "Turn your eyes upon Jesus. Look full in his wonderful face, and the things of earth will grow strangely dim, in the light of his glory and grace." When we look only to the Lord, all comparison will drop away.

Heavenly Father, I pray you will help me overcome overcome comparison with the transformative power your love brings. I will anchor my worth in your affirmation and cultivate a grateful heart that makes you smile. I am enough because you are more than enough. Amen.

Lord, I am so thankful for the life you have given me today.

DAY 13

The Power of Gratitude

Do all things without complaining and disputing, that you may become blameless.
PHILIPPIANS 2:14–15 NKJV

Sometimes when I read the story of the Israelites wandering in the desert with Moses, I marvel at their foolishness. How could they witness the incredible power of God in one moment and then complain soon after? But then I take a step back and realize—I've done the same thing. In today's verse, God reminds us not to complain. When we do, we are living outside of God's plan for our lives.

Believers who constantly grumble risk entangling themselves in negativity. Proverbs 21:9 vividly depicts the corrosive nature of a complaining spirit: "Better to live on a corner of the roof than share a house with a quarrelsome wife" (NIV). Complaining corrodes relationships, dampens joy, and erodes peace within a household, community, ministry, or organization. A complaining spirit, like a constant dripping, wears away at the foundations of love, unity, and harmony. It is a subtle but destructive force that demands vigilance.

Psalm 107:1 reminds us to always give thanks. This is the antidote to a complaining spirit. When we focus on God's blessings, we foster an environment where God's will can flourish. Gratitude is a powerful tool to combat negativity and redirect our heart toward the source of all goodness and truth. Colossians 3:17 invites believers to recognize that everything we do is for God: "Whatever you do, whether in word or deed, do it all in the name of the Lord Jesus, giving thanks to God the Father through him" (NIV).

We must turn to God in prayer and gratitude. Turning to God in prayer will not only guard us against complaining, but it will also help us understand God's mind and stay aligned with his heart. Turning to the Lord daily will keep our minds renewed and our perspective clear. The world is full of filth, so we must wash our minds in intimate conversation with him. We cannot become blameless on our own. We need to ask God for help. When we open ourselves to him, he will remind us of his elaborate goodness, infinite grace, and extraordinary kindness. And isn't that so much better than complaining?

When we spend time with the Lord, it's important to be honest with him. We should bring our concerns to

God with a thankful heart, remembering his power and provision. When we complain, we are only focused on earthly problems, while gratitude keeps our focus on God's goodness. His resources are unlimited. Even in the darkest circumstances, he will provide for us, his children. A heart filled with trust and thanksgiving will let us navigate any challenges the devil may throw at us.

Psalm 100:4 encourages believers to "enter his gates with thanksgiving and his courts with praise; give thanks to him and praise his name" (NIV). Instead of complaining, what if the Israelites had thanked the Lord for his goodness and worshiped joyfully as they journeyed through the desert? The story of their exodus from Egypt would have been one of abundant blessings, and they could have immediately entered the promised land instead of perishing in the wilderness, where they wandered for decades.

The Bible is filled with stories of people who didn't complain when challenges arose and who instead journeyed through life filled with gratitude and worship unto the Lord. I pray that our lives will reflect those of Hezekiah, Ruth, Paul, and so many more. A grateful mindset will help us walk in God's light, focusing on his will rather than our circumstances. Psalm 118:24 encourages believers to make a daily choice: "This is the day that the Lord has made; let us rejoice and be glad in it" (ESV). May we always delight in the Lord, no matter what.

Father, teach me to know your will. Help me embrace the transformative power of gratitude rather than complain about the circumstances in which you have placed me. You bless my life, Lord. May I bless your heart as well. Amen.

My lips shall not complain so that I can fully enjoy your peace and radiantly witness your goodness in every circumstance.

DAY 14

Who Told You That?

"My sheep hear my voice,
and I know them,
and they follow me."
JOHN 10:27 ESV

Before jumping into today's verse, turn the page all the way back to Genesis 3:11, where God posed a question to Adam that has reverberated through the ages: "Who told you that you were naked?" (NIV). God wasn't just asking Adam where he got this information. He was reminding us to be discerning about whose voice we listen to every day. Are we attuned to the voice of God, or are we swayed by the whispers of the Enemy?

Satan speaks negative and destructive messages about us, seeking to undermine our confidence, worth, and identity in Christ. He preys on our insecurities and feelings of inadequacy. He pesters you with lies, saying that you will never change, that freedom is not fully available to you, and that you are alone and unlovable. Do not ever listen to these false whispers.

Instead, turn to God's truth. We are fearfully and wonderfully made, loved unconditionally by our heavenly Father, and redeemed by the precious blood of Jesus Christ. He is waiting with outstretched arms, longing for us to run to him so he can hold us fast. When we cling to the truth of God's Word, we silence the Enemy's lies and walk in the freedom and victory that Christ has secured for us.

God's love for us is tightly woven throughout the entire Bible. In Romans 5:8, God reminds us that he loved us so much that he sent his Son to die for us. First John 3:1 declares that we are not just servants of God—we are his children. Turn to 1 Peter 2:9 to see that we are his chosen people whom he called out of darkness and into his light.

Countless verses speak life, hope, freedom, and victory over our lives. These passages remind us of our true identity and worth in Christ and empower us to live boldly and confidently as children of God. These words must be so immovable within our spirit that when another voice comes to whisper anything different, we refuse it and rebuke the lies in Jesus' name.

It can be challenging to hold on to the truth in a world filled with competing voices clamoring for our attention, but the quality of our faith depends on whose word we believe. So how do we tell if we are hearing the voice of God or the voice of the Enemy? We cultivate a relationship with God. Just as Adam walked with God in the garden, we must walk with our Creator through all the trials and challenges of this life. Through prayer, worship, and fellowship with other believers, we open our heart to hear his voice more clearly.

Today's verse tells us that we are God's sheep and that he is our Shepherd. Sheep recognize and respond to the voice of their shepherd, and we must recognize and respond to the voice of our Shepherd. Only then can we trust in his guidance and follow him faithfully no matter what life throws at us. God has a great plan for our lives. To live it out, we must follow his voice.

Whenever you are struggling with doubt, ask yourself, "Who told me that?" Are you listening to the voice of God, whose declarations bring life, truth, and love? Or are you succumbing to the lies of the Enemy, whose whispers breed fear, doubt, and division? Strive to hear the difference between God's voice and the devil's. When you hear your Shepherd speak, listen and follow.

Father, in the name of Jesus, I pray that I will always attune my heart and mind to your voice. I thank you for the truth you speak to me through your Word. I will live my life according to your truth. In Jesus' name. Amen.

My life will reflect the voice that I believe.

DAY 15

Do You Want to Be Healed?

When Jesus saw him lying there and knew that
he had already been there a long time, he said to him,
"Do you want to be healed?"
JOHN 5:6 ESV

The man in today's verse had been unable to walk for thirty-eight years. This is difficult by today's standards, and it was even harder during Jesus' time, when there weren't surgeries to help him get better or even wheelchairs to help him move around. So instead of living his life, he lay by the pool of Bethesda, hoping for a miracle to make him well. But when his miracle finally arrived, he was too stuck in self-pity to realize it (John 5:7).

If we focus only on our problems, hopelessness will

creep in and trap us in self-pity. But Philippians 2:3–4 says, "Do nothing out of selfish ambition or vain conceit. Rather, in humility value others above yourselves, not looking to your own interests but each of you to the interests of the others" (NIV). Self-pity arises from focusing on our own problems, neglecting the needs and interests of others, and seeking attention instead of growth.

When we are hurting, it is perfectly normal for us to want others to commiserate with us. Of course we want to feel supported. However, falling into the temptation of self-pity can trap our heart and hinder our spiritual development. When we are too comfortable in our state of despair, it becomes nearly impossible to exercise our faith and choose to trust and believe in God's plan. Self-pity zaps out of us the spiritual sensitivity required to recognize the miracles present in the toughest moments of our lives.

If we don't recognize God's miracles, we can't receive them. God has positioned us to be victors, not victims. This is the only road to true recovery and healing.

Second Corinthians 1:3–4 acknowledges God as the ultimate source of comfort:

> Praise be to the God and Father of our Lord Jesus Christ, the Father of compassion and the God of all comfort, who comforts us in all our troubles, so that we can comfort those in any trouble with the comfort we ourselves receive from God. (NIV)

True comfort comes from God, not from the deceptive comfort of self-pity. Instead of finding acceptance and attention in self-pity, we as believers are called to turn to the Father of compassion, who offers genuine comfort and real and lasting healing.

Immediately after meeting the lame man, the first thing Jesus asked him was "Do you want to be healed?" This question confronted the man's victim mindset right from the start. Jesus didn't bother with small talk. He didn't even respond to the man's answer, which was spoken from a world of selfishness and misery. Instead, he cut straight to the command to "rise, take up your bed and walk" (John 5:8 NKJV). This was a moment of decision for this man. Would he continue to complain, or would he act in faith that would lead him toward a new reality? Jesus' response to the man was one of compassion and power. Jesus' command not only restored his physical health but also shattered the chains of victimhood that had bound him for so long.

In the same way, Jesus calls us to rise up from our brokenness, to leave behind the victim mentality that holds us captive, and to walk boldly into the new identity he prepared for us. This identity through Christ allows us to step out into a world of endless possibilities of healing, freedom, and wholeness in Jesus' name. Just as this man chose to trust Jesus, picked up his mat, and walked, we, too, should get up, lift our heads out of our own problems, and trust in God's victorious plan for our lives.

Father, in the name of Jesus, I vow to renew my mind with your truth and reject the false narrative of self-pity that keeps me bound and broken. I long to embrace the truth of my victorious identity in you. Align my thoughts with your Word so I can break free from the chains of self-pity and walk in the freedom of your truth. Amen.

Lord, I receive your healing. I declare that I am well and made whole in Jesus' name.

DAY 16

Surrendering to Jesus

Trust in the Lord with all thine heart;
and lean not unto thine own understanding.
Proverbs 3:5 KJV

Relinquishing control is not something that most of us enjoy. I have often stood in church, belting out the words to the hymn "I Surrender All" while holding on tightly to my life, barely recognizing my own hypocrisy. I'm a planner, so surrendering my plans to walk with a faith-focused God has had its rocky moments. Whenever I long to cling to my plans, I remind myself that, as God's creation, I never really had any control in the first place. He is the creator of the universe, and we must trust in his sovereign plan for our life.

The temptation to rely on our own understanding instead of trusting in the Lord is rooted in fear. We are afraid that God won't do what we want. We want to control the timing of our lives rather than leave it up to him. The next time you are scared to give up control, turn to God's reminder in Isaiah 55:8–9:

> "My thoughts are not your thoughts, neither are your ways my ways," declares the LORD. "As the heavens are higher than the earth, so are my ways higher than your ways and my thoughts than your thoughts." (NIV)

And don't forget God's promise in 2 Timothy 1:7 to those who surrender fear: "God has not given us a spirit of fear, but of power and of love and of a sound mind" (NKJV). The Lord eagerly waits to help us lay all anxious thoughts at his feet. Every fear of the unknown, fear of failure, and fear of disappointment.

I realized that I needed to humble myself and acknowledge that I didn't have enough knowledge or understanding to control everything. God has considered my past, present, and future. He completely understands me, far better than I understand myself. He has a panoramic view of every situation and knows the outcome. This is why placing our lives in God's hands will always yield lasting fruit. God's ways exceed our understanding, so when we surrender our need for control, we acknowledge our limitations and entrust our lives to the one whose ways are perfect.

Philippians 4:6–7 assures believers of the peace that comes with surrender:

> Do not be anxious about anything, but in every situation, by prayer and petition, with thanksgiving, present your requests to God. And the peace of God, which transcends all understanding, will guard your hearts and your minds in Christ Jesus. (NIV)

God wants us to have peace. When we cling to our old lives, we do so out of fear of the unknown. We can never receive God's peace when we're carrying heavy burdens we weren't meant to carry.

Controlling our own lives is stressful. When we ignore God, we have no way of knowing what path to walk down. In fact, without God, our only option is to use our very limited understanding to figure out the course of our life. This is a needless burden to bear when God invites us to turn to him and receive his direction, and he will give us rest. When we are determined to trust in Christ, we will receive the beautiful gift of stress-relieving peace and joy that's hard to explain.

We can't surrender ourselves to God without his help. We have to pray and ask God for the power to release our need for immediate control. Remember Ecclesiastes 3:1, which says, "There is a time for everything, and a season for every activity under the heavens" (NIV). Once you realize that God's timing is impeccable, the urgency to control your life will begin to decrease. Defeat control with trust.

Father, thank you for taking my hand and leading me to a place of surrender. Instead of anxiety and the relentless need for control, I can present my requests with thanksgiving. Let your peace become a guard for my heart and mind. Amen.

What a blessed gift that I don't have to carry heavy loads. I get to surrender it all to you.

DAY 17

What's on Your Mind?

Do not love the world or anything in the world. If anyone loves the world, love for the Father is not in them.
1 JOHN 2:15 NIV

We are constantly bombarded with information from news, podcasts, talk shows, social media, billboards, and more. Each distraction offers a different opinion, one message clashing with another. It can be difficult to discern the truth. To align ourselves with God's perspective, we must focus on renewing our minds through his Word, even in the midst of worldly influences. Romans 12:2 lays the foundation for our Christian journey:

> Do not conform to the pattern of this world, but be transformed by the renewing of your mind. Then you will be able to test and approve what God's will is—his good, pleasing and perfect will. (NIV)

To discern God's will, we must always battle against the world, cleaning our minds of its influences.

1 John 2:15–16 cautions believers about the allure of the world:

> Do not love the world or anything in the world. If anyone loves the world, love for the Father is not in them. For everything in the world—the lust of the flesh, the lust of the eyes, and the pride of life—comes not from the Father but from the world. (NIV)

The world entices us with fleeting pleasures—materialism, worldly beauty, and temporary success. Falling for these traps is easier than keeping our eyes trained on heaven.

We must remain watchful. Our role as Christians is to discern what is of God and what is not. We need to intentionally shift our focus from the temporary to the eternal and resist the allure that leads us away from God.

The only way to resist is through the transformative power of God's Word:

> The word of God is alive and active. Sharper than any double-edged sword, it penetrates even to dividing soul and spirit, joints and marrow; it judges the thoughts and attitudes of the heart. (Hebrews 4:12 NIV)

The Bible is not just a book. It is powerful, fully active, and immeasurably potent. When we eat and drink from its pages daily, transformation is inevitable.

In 2020, the United States was drenched in arguments, distrust, and fear. Depression and anxiety reached an all-time high. Friends and family fought over history and politics. Everywhere I looked, Satan's power flourished. Unfortunately, this was nothing new. Satan has always used fear and hate to strengthen his control over the earth.

But 2 Corinthians 10:5 teaches us how to overcome hate with God's glory: "We demolish arguments and every pretension that sets itself up against the knowledge of God, and we take captive every thought to make it obedient to Christ" (NIV). The mind is a battleground for doubt, fear, and self-condemnation. To renew the mind is to take every thought captive, aligning it with the knowledge of God and making it obedient to Christ.

This world wants you to be anxious and fearful, lonely and desperate. But Colossians 3:2 encourages you to "set your minds on things above, not on earthly things" (NIV). God calls you to a kingdom perspective. This is a game changer. Instead of a mindset of fear, receive God's mindset of peace that surpasses all understanding.

We must be intentional about spending time with God, especially when the social climate is flooded with new ideologies and opposing beliefs. We read the Word not to check it off our list for the day but to truly allow his powerful Word and presence to permeate our hearts and minds so we can be washed in his perspective.

Dear Father, forgive me for all idle thoughts, arguments, and behaviors that do not align with your kingdom principles. Show me how to live in this world without being consumed by it so that I can be a shining light for your glory on this earth. Amen.

With your kingdom perspective, I can discern the difference between the valuable and the worthless things of this world.

DAY 18

Set Apart for His Glory

It is written, Be ye holy; for I am holy.
1 PETER 1:16 KJV

What is holiness? Some people think that it means wearing long skirts and avoiding makeup and jewelry. Others believe that it involves refraining from sin and following rigid rules. But holiness is much deeper and richer than these superficial ideas. It is a reflection of God's nature. Nothing we can do will make us holy. We only become holy through God's presence in our lives.

Holiness means wholeness. To say that "God is holy" is to refer to the wholeness, fullness, beauty, and abundant life that overflows within the Trinity. God lacks nothing. He is unbroken, undamaged, unfallen. He is the indivisible One, wholly self-sufficient, the picture of perfection. When the Bible says that God is holy, it means that he is perfect and complete.

It is difficult to imagine such a complete healing in

such a broken world. But light brilliantly shines in the darkness. Just as the holy God can exist in this fallen world, we can become like him and reflect his glory to the people around us. When Jesus the Holy One exhorted us to "be perfect," he was inviting us to a life of wholeness and holiness (Matthew 5:48 NKJV). The Greek word for *perfect* means "finished" or "complete."[3] Jesus was saying, "Be complete as your Father in heaven is complete."

It is a beautiful thing to live a life that is set apart for the Lord. As believers, we are encouraged to avoid destructive habits because they smear the stain of sin upon our hearts and minds that need to be clean before the Lord. Satan celebrates destruction, so under his guidance, the world will lead us down these sinful paths.

But the Lord invites us to be set apart. When we avoid unclean things, we will experience peace and purpose in God's presence. We will long for a deep, intimate relationship with God as his beloved sons and daughters. Our lives will be testaments to the saving and sustaining power of God. Under his power, we will conquer the Enemy and experience God's glorious victory.

God calls us to be holy and clean at all times. Philippians 4:8 states: "Brothers and sisters, whatever is true, whatever is noble, whatever is right, whatever is pure, whatever is lovely, whatever is admirable—if

---

3 Strong, *Strong's Expanded Exhaustive Concordance of the Bible*, G5046.

anything is excellent or praiseworthy—think about such things" (NIV). But when the news reports that children are starving, how can we think about excellence? When a family member is diagnosed with cancer, how do we sing praise? Only through the Lord.

Self-pity and anger at the world have no place in the heart and mind of a believer, but we cannot overcome them without God's help. If we come to God, surrendering our feelings, he will heal us and make us whole. God can turn even the most broken person into a holy reflection of his glory. Through him, all things are possible.

Isn't that amazing? God loves us so deeply that he wants us to be like him, look like him, and sound like him. He has promised to supply all our needs according to his endless riches. Through the beauty of his holiness, we are covered on every side and supported by an all-powerful Father. Holiness is not oppressive. It is a gift! We get to be surrounded by his refreshing comfort, provision, and purity. We don't have to partake in the life-damaging ideologies, addictions, and strongholds that bring trauma, confusion, brokenness, and sin. God has provided another option—a life that is free and filled with love.

The world is searching for real, sustainable peace and joy. Let us share our holiness with others.

Father, today I embrace the beautiful and sacred gift of perfection and completion. Thank you, Jesus, that I get to be holy as you are holy! Hallelujah! Amen.

I give you praise and honor for your incredible love that makes me whole.

DAY 19

A Woman of Courageous Influence

Who knoweth whether thou art come to the kingdom for such a time as this?

Esther 4:14 kjv

Esther's story began in the land of Persia, where she emerged as a woman thrust into a position of influence during a critical time. Esther 2:17 describes her ascent:

> The king loved Esther more than all the women, and she won grace and favor in his sight more than all the virgins, so that he set the royal crown on her head and made her queen. (ESV)

Esther was orphaned and raised by her cousin Mordecai, forced to marry a man she didn't know, and kept separate from her people. She couldn't even let the king know who she truly was. But through these horrific challenges, even when her identity seemed stolen from her, Esther embraced her identity in God and remained strong and courageous in her faith.

Courage can be defined as the ability to confront fear, pain, danger, uncertainty, or intimidation. It's not the absence of fear but rather the strength to act despite our fear. Courage often involves taking risks or facing challenges for a greater good or a noble cause. Jesus was courageous, and he wants us to be courageous as well. Why? Because the spirit of fear is a thief. It keeps us immobile when the Lord is calling us to trust him and move forward. Fear will keep us from experiencing God's glorious miracles.

Generations upon generations are grateful that Esther didn't give in to fear. When Mordecai begged Queen Esther to do something about Haman's destructive decree, she explained that she could lose her life if she approached the king without his summons (Esther 4:11). Mordecai responded by reminding her why she became queen. With God's leading, Esther risked her life by going before the king unsummoned.

Whenever we are too afraid to move forward, we must remember that we have a protector who is always with us. Isaiah 41:10 says, "Fear not, for I am with you; be not dismayed, for I am your God; I will strengthen you, I will help you, I will uphold you with my righteous right hand" (ESV). We should also remember that our courageous actions will impact others. The Bible is filled with ordinary people who spoke up and took action in the face of fear. Those are the people who changed the world.

Esther wasn't anyone special by earthly standards. She was an orphan, a normal girl from a simple town, just doing her best to live according to God's will. But God chose her to save his people from annihilation, and he can choose us too. Embrace your identity in Christ and prepare yourself to take a stand in faith.

The best way to do this is to live in communion with God, praying and reading his Word daily. Before speaking to the king, Esther asked her people to join her in praying and fasting for three days. When we invest ourselves in God's Word, we will come to understand his thoughts and desires. We will want to follow only God's plan because it is the safest and most fruitful option for our lives. In Matthew 4:4, Jesus declared, "Man shall not live by bread alone, but by every word that comes from the mouth of God" (ESV). As we follow his leading, our lives will reflect the beauty of who he is. This, my friend, is how we live a deeply fulfilling and purposeful life.

We may be cast out by this world or suffer persecution for the Lord. Yet still we are called to take action, to use the skills God has given us in the battle for our families, communities, nation, and world.

Being bold and courageous for one's faith doesn't always mean facing life-threatening situations. It can also involve everyday acts of kindness, compassion, and integrity that reflect our dedication to following the teachings of Christ.

Are you willing to follow the Lord far outside your comfort zone to take risks that will transform the lives of others? Remember, with God, all things are possible. He will call you to do great things according to his glorious purpose. Be ready.

Father, thank you for helping me to do the hard things. Lord, I surrender my desire for self-preservation and proclaim that my life is yours. Perform your will through me. Amen.

The Lord stands ready to increase my courage, boldness, and determination to fulfill his call.

DAY 20

From Brokenness to Redemption

The LORD is close to the brokenhearted
and saves those who are crushed in spirit.
PSALM 34:18 NIV

My parents divorced after twenty-five years of marriage. I was an adult, and I remember feeling as if I were grieving a death. My family was fragmenting, my foundations shaking. I was heartbroken. How do young children cope with it? I was grown and could barely stay seated in my emotional rollercoaster.

My family was close growing up. My parents were friendly, respected, and ministry oriented. We hosted guests and fed college students. Some people even called us the "Cosby Show family" because we were funny and loved playing music and games with our guests. Now we were broken and hurting beyond words.

I kept my emotions bottled up, hoping to control my anguish. But one day while cleaning my house, I dropped the broom and yelled, “Lord, I’m so angry!” The floodgates opened, and I fell to the floor weeping. But as the tears came, a sense of peace and assurance washed over me. Now I could begin the process of true healing because I was honest about my emotions. I needed to acknowledge my brokenness before God and recognize that it was the starting point for his redemptive work.

If you have a broken heart or spirit and have been crushed by your circumstances, remember that God draws near to those who recognize their need for him. Second Corinthians 12:9–10 speaks to the strength found in weakness:

> He said to me, “My grace is sufficient for you, for my power is made perfect in weakness.” Therefore I will boast all the more gladly about my weaknesses, so that Christ’s power may rest on me. That is why, for Christ’s sake, I delight in weaknesses, in insults, in hardships, in persecutions, in difficulties. For when I am weak, then I am strong. (NIV)

We must find strength by acknowledging our weaknesses.

This paradox leaves me overwhelmingly impressed by God. He is the only one who can make all things work together for my good in every situation. God's power is strongest when we are weakest; his grace and mercy abound in places we would never imagine. Instead of hiding our weakness or brokenness, we can boast in it, knowing that it becomes the canvas on which God paints his redemptive masterpiece.

It is not for any of us to try to figure out the how. We just need to trust in God's ability to restore the years that seem lost. Just as the grass turns green and trees bear fruit each spring after a season of winter, God will bring forth abundance in us after a season of sadness. God's redemptive work is not just about recovery. He also offers abundance beyond anything we could imagine.

Psalm 30:11–12 captures the essence of God's redemptive power: "You turned my wailing into dancing; you removed my sackcloth and clothed me with joy, that my heart may sing your praises and not be silent. Lord my God, I will praise you forever" (NIV). God works in our brokenness when we turn to him. He is our great healer; he will turn our mourning into joy!

In your seasons of darkness, turn to God. Only through him can we learn to offer forgiveness to those who have hurt us and move on in faith. We might not understand our circumstances, but God does. When you can't see what is around the corner, close your eyes and trust God to guide your steps.

Father, thank you for walking with me through the toughest moments of my life. I surrender my emotions and acknowledge my feelings so that you can teach me how to find strength in you. Even in life's darkness, you make all things work together for my good. Amen.

You will lead me to a place where mourning turns into dancing and where wailing is replaced with joy.

DAY 21

The Importance of Rest

Come unto me, all ye that labour and are heavy laden, and I will give you rest.
MATTHEW 11:28 KJV

Rest is challenging. Our culture values hard work and success, neither of which are bad things. God wants us to work hard. But he also wants us to rest, just as he rested on the seventh day.

Genesis 2:2–3 reflects on God's rest after creation:

> By the seventh day God had finished the work he had been doing; so on the seventh day he rested from all his work. Then God blessed the seventh day and made it holy, because on it he rested from all the work of creating that he had done. (NIV)

I love talking about God's power, love, favor, healing, provision, and authority, but I often overlook the importance of rest. God leads by example and does everything intentionally. Even though he doesn't necessarily need to rest, he wants to show us how important it is to take a day of rest away from the busyness of life.

When was the last time resting was on your to-do list? When the whole world says to stay busy, resting feels like a waste of time. Like we are missing opportunities or failing to be successful. According to the world, rest simply is not valuable.

God created us with a need for the Sabbath, a day that's not only a time of physical rest but a sacred time for reflection and communion with the Lord. In embracing Sabbath rest, believers enter a rhythm that mirrors God's own restful completion. When we choose to rest, we trust that God will take care of our needs. We show our knowledge of his ultimate control over all our work. Resting shows our dependence on him and reveals that we believe he's got us.

When the psalmist says, "Rest in the LORD, and wait patiently for Him" (Psalm 37:7 NKJV), he's not talking about physical rest like taking a nap. Physical rest is important, but even more importantly, we need spiritual rest from the weights of this world—confusion, worry, stress, anxiety, and weariness. We must be at peace in our body and soul.

In place of "rest in the LORD," some Bible translations say, "Be still before the LORD" (NIV), "Be silent before the LORD" (CSB), "Surrender yourself to the

Lord" (GW), or "Be still in the presence of the Lord" (NLT). To rest spiritually, we must dwell in the presence of the Lord and be willing to surrender all our busy thoughts, anxieties, worries, and frustrations. We should go to him and offer our heavy burdens, for he promises to give us the rest we need (Matthew 11:28–30).

God designed physical rest to allow our bodies to recuperate from the demands of daily life. During sleep, our bodies repair tissues, regulate hormones, and strengthen the immune system, contributing to overall health. Just as physical rest rejuvenates the body, resting in God rejuvenates the spirit. Spending time in prayer, meditation, and communion with God nourishes our soul, bringing refreshment, peace, and spiritual renewal.

At times, I am not even aware of how exhausted I am until I sit down and take a break. God understands our human limitations. He knows that we need rest to be physically and spiritually healthy. Maybe it's time to take a step back and evaluate yourself. What heavy emotions or spiritual weights are you carrying today?

Dear sisters, I urge you to accept the divine invitation to come to Jesus with all your burdens. Even if you think you don't need rest, it is important to take a break and look for restoration in the gentle and humble heart of Jesus. When we find refuge in him, the weight of our challenges will be replaced with the restful ease of his presence. What a glorious exchange this is!

Father, I pray that I will not be anxious about anything, but in every situation, by prayer and petition, with thanksgiving, present my requests to you. I pray that your incredible peace, which transcends my understanding, will guard my heart and mind in Christ Jesus. Amen.

Lord, I will rest in you. There I know I will find refreshment that will revive my soul and spirit.

DAY 22

The Grace to Apologize

Humble yourselves in the sight of the Lord,
and he shall lift you up.
JAMES 4:10 KJV

I deeply enjoy apologizing—said no one ever! To apologize, we need to acknowledge that we were wrong, which requires humility and remorse. Neither are very comfortable feelings. But as Christians, we understand that we are not perfect and that asking for forgiveness is an unavoidable part of our lives.

In today's verse, God calls us to humble ourselves before him. Humility can seem like a sign of weakness, but in reality, it is a powerful virtue of God that leads to divine strength.

It took an immense amount of humility for the almighty God to take on the form of a tiny human baby and be born of a young woman into the humblest of circumstances. He entered the frailty of mortality and was laid in a trough that was used for feeding animals. To top it all off, he came to die for a people that, for the most part, would reject him. If God can humble himself, then we must be willing to do the same.

Philippians 2:5–7 says,

> Indeed, let this attitude be in you, which was also in Christ Jesus. Though he was by nature God, he did not consider equality with God as a prize to be displayed, but he emptied himself by taking the nature of a servant. When he was born in human likeness, and his appearance was like that of any other man. (EHV)

Apologizing requires a humble heart. We must acknowledge our imperfections and rely on God's grace to guide us through the process. Only then can we be lifted up to be with God.

Notice this biblical parallel: when you humble yourself, you are lifted up. When Jesus was crucified—the ultimate humbling—he was lifted up on the cross. When we are humble on earth, we will be raised up in heaven. Since Jesus was willing to humble himself, we can now follow his example and receive his victory, where we will be reunited with God in heaven. We are no longer at the mercy of fear, death, and the grave. Jesus has conquered the Enemy.

But none of this would have happened without humility. One of the biggest obstacles to humbling ourselves and sincerely apologizing is pride. Proverbs

16:18 warns against pride: "Pride goes before destruction, a haughty spirit before a fall" (NIV). This perfectly describes Satan. He was so full of pride that he desired to be like God and consequently was cast out of heaven. Only through Jesus' humility and sacrifice on the cross was Satan's pride defeated. We are called to be like God, not like Satan. Pride is toxic and poisonous to the soul. As believers, we must avoid it at all costs.

Colossians 3:12–13 explains that we must forgive others with humility as well:

> As God's chosen people, holy and dearly loved, clothe yourselves with compassion, kindness, humility, gentleness and patience. Bear with each other and forgive one another if any of you has a grievance against someone. Forgive as the Lord forgave you. (NIV)

When we clothe ourselves in humility, we put others before ourselves, whether apologizing for how we have hurt them or forgiving them for how they have hurt us. We recognize that the cares of this world don't matter. We begin to look more like God.

At the core of humility lies love—love for others, love for God, and love for his Word. This love enables us to undertake even the most difficult tasks, knowing that it will please the Lord. First Corinthians 13:4–7 provides a detailed description of the attributes of love:

> Love is patient, love is kind. It does not envy, it does not boast, it is not proud. It does not dishonor others, it is not self-seeking, it is not easily angered, it keeps no record of wrongs. Love does not delight in evil but rejoices with the truth. It always protects, always trusts, always hopes, always perseveres. (NIV)

Everything we will ever need to stay free in Christ is rooted in love.

Father, I come to you confessing my sins and humbling myself before you. Lord, please give me the humility to apologize to anyone I've hurt. Help me find healing and peace in you. In Jesus' name. Amen.

Show me through the Holy Spirit whom I need to apologize to.

DAY 23

Rediscovering the Father's Heart

The Son can do nothing of himself,
but what he seeth the Father do:
for what things soever he doeth,
these also doeth the Son likewise.
JOHN 5:19 KJV

The first time I read through the whole Bible, I came away with the impression that Jesus and the Father were quite different. While God the Father seemed strict, no-nonsense, and disciplinary, Jesus was kind, merciful, and loving. As I read about the various times God the Father brought judgment upon the people of Israel, I began to view him in much the same way that I viewed my earthly father. My father was an excellent dad, but he was also the disciplinarian in our home, and it was easy to overlook his love for me and only see his rules.

I didn't realize until later that I had combined my earthly father's traits with my heavenly Father's. Just as I had done with my dad, I was ignoring God's love for me and focusing on the rules. This is a common practice among many believers. Many young people I know today have trouble accepting God's love because of difficulties in their relationships with their earthly fathers.

Our understanding of our heavenly Father forms the foundation of our beliefs and practices. When we don't understand who he is, we won't be able to understand his Word. Many relationships fail because people do not take the time to get to know one another deeply. We need to take the time to get to know our heavenly Father to maintain our relationship with him. We need to reevaluate our view of God and recognize the perfect harmony of love and kindness found in both the Father and the Son.

As I got older, I started to delve into the Scriptures to better understand the Father's heart. As I did, I realized that I had many misconceptions. I used to think that the Old Testament only talked about the Father and the New Testament only talked about Jesus. However, I came to understand that Jesus is revealed throughout the Old Testament and that the Father's heart is displayed through the life of Jesus in the New Testament. In fact, the entire Bible is full of instances where the Father and Son's oneness is evident, as well as their shared love and compassion for humanity.

In today's verse, Jesus clearly shows us how the motives, heart, desires, and actions of both the Father and Son are one. Even though they are separate beings at this moment, they are still the same God. The love that Jesus feels in his heart, God feels also. John 14:9 is another verse that displays how inseparable the Father and Son are. "Jesus said to him, 'Have I been with you so long, and you still do not know me, Philip? Whoever has seen me has seen the Father'" (ESV). God and Jesus are one and the same God, the God who loves you enough to sacrifice himself to save you.

My favorite story in the Bible is the parable of the prodigal son in Luke 15:11–32. This story beautifully illustrates the Father's response to a wayward child. The father in this story didn't yell at his prodigal son; he didn't punish him severely. Instead, he ran toward the returning son with open arms, expressing joy and lavish mercy.

God's heart is crying for us to return to him. He is not harsh and unforgiving. He's waiting for us with open arms so he can throw a party at our return. I pray that we examine our understanding of our heavenly Father's perfect love and dispel any fear that may arise from misconceptions. As we align our hearts with the truth revealed in Christ, we can love and trust the

Father without reservation, knowing that his character is defined by the purest love.

Father, thank you for your grace as you help me understand who you are. Holy Spirit, I ask you to help me to release all misconceptions. You, God, are greater than anyone on this earth, and I must not compare your glory to our sinfulness. It is my great pleasure to read your Word and spend time in your presence so I can get to know you better each day. Amen.

Every relationship in my life must be built on truth and truth alone.

DAY 24

A Woman of Godly Leadership

Deborah, a prophetess, the wife of Lapidoth, she judged Israel at that time.
JUDGES 4:4 KJV

Have you ever found yourself in a situation where you were offered a new job or a leadership role but you felt unprepared or inadequate to take on the challenge? The first time I was asked to sing in the background for a well-known Christian artist, my knees shook. Could I really do it well? I accepted the position, but I did not feel at all adequate.

Many times I have been fortunate enough to be presented with amazing opportunities, and while I was happy on the outside, inside I was nervous and praying for help. However, I believe that God opens doors for a reason and wants to work with us to do extraordinary things on earth. With his help, we can achieve great things. My prayer is that we never get in the way of what God wants to do in our lives.

During Deborah's time, the people of Israel had once again turned their backs on the Lord and, as a result, lived under the oppressive hand of Jabin, king of Canaan. Deborah stands out as the only female judge mentioned in the Bible. She is also one of only five women mentioned as prophets in the Old Testament.

Deborah's resume included prolific poet, prophetess, songwriter, singer and worshiper, warrior, military leader, and wife—totally demolishing the idea that you can only do and be one thing to be successful. By his grace, God gave her all the skills and roles she needed to fulfill her call on the earth.

In Judges 4:9, Bar'ak asked her to go with him into battle. She replied, "I will surely go with you; nevertheless there will be no glory for you in the journey you are taking, for the Lord will sell Sisera into the hand of a woman" (NKJV). Women in ancient Israel did not usually fight in wars, but God gave her the strength not just to fight but to win the battle.

Sometimes the Lord may call us to do something we feel powerless to accomplish. However, God is with us, just like he was with Deborah. When God calls you to act, he will equip you with everything you need (Hebrews 13:20–21). Despite the challenges and uncertainties, Deborah embraced her role with unwavering faith. We are also called to trust God's leading, even when the path ahead seems daunting.

As we work to fulfill God's glory, we must stop and give him praise for equipping us. After the Israelites won the battle, Deborah stopped and sang praises to the Lord. I encourage you to read Judges 5, which recounts Deborah's song of praise. In this anthem, she acknowledged God's role in the triumph and highlighted the contributions of those who participated in the battle. A true God-fearing leader knows their limitations and praises God for working even in their weakness.

When God opens a door for you, walk through it confidently, knowing that God sent you there. You will feel inadequate. God doesn't call us to do easy tasks. But you must receive the Lord's adequacy and keep putting one foot in front of the other. The Lord will display his glory through your trust and faith in him.

Father, thank you for Deborah's story that teaches me about courage, leadership, and faith. Just as Deborah led with wisdom and worship, may I, too, faithfully accomplish the tasks you give me. Help me to recognize that you work through all people, no matter how small or weak, to fulfill your glorious purposes. Amen.

There are no limits on whom God will partner with or what he can do. He is the Lord.

DAY 25

The Modern Proverbs 31 Woman

Who can find a virtuous woman?
for her price is far above rubies.
PROVERBS 31:10 KJV

When I first moved to Nashville to attend college, I met a beautiful woman who feared God with all her heart. She was graceful and wise, and every time I was around her, she made me laugh. She partnered with her husband in ministry, and she battled the Enemy in prayer every day. But what intrigued me the most about her was the way she loved the Lord. In her, I saw what I wanted in my life: a love for the Lord that surpassed all understanding.

At the time, I was insecure about my worth and desperately wanted to understand God's purpose for my life. I knew that this real-life Proverbs 31 woman could guide me in the right direction. One day, I gathered the courage to ask her to be my mentor. She kindly agreed. Without her mentorship, I would not be the woman I am today.

Although King Solomon wrote this description of a godly woman thousands of years ago, these qualities still stand true today. The Proverbs 31 woman in today's world is a woman of strength, grace, and purpose. She blesses her household and community. She faces challenges with faithful confidence, and she understands her identity in Christ.

She is a wise and resourceful manager: "She considers a field and buys it; with the fruit of her hands she plants a vineyard" (v. 16 ESV). We may not be regularly buying fields any longer, but we do need to manage our careers, finances, and households. Organization requires careful consideration and strategic planning. We need to invest our time and talents wisely to steward the gifts God has given us.

She is compassionate and generous: "She opens her hand to the poor and reaches out her hands to the needy" (v. 20 ESV). This does not include just financial generosity; we must also share our time, wisdom, and encouragement. What good things God has given us, we must share with others.

She speaks kindly with wisdom: "She opens her mouth with wisdom, and the teaching of kindness is on her tongue" (v. 26 ESV). A godly woman speaks godliness to those around her. We are called to patience and kindness at all times. We must search the Bible for wisdom to use in our own lives and to share with others.

She fears the Lord above all else: "Charm is deceitful, and beauty is vain, but a woman who fears the LORD is to be praised" (v. 30 ESV). This quality is the most important of all. Beauty and charm may seem like good things, but they will not last. Our confidence must stem from our fear of the Lord, for he defines our worth. Only then will we become true women of God.

Does this feel impossible? At first glance, the woman described here seems too perfect, someone who could never truly exist. But God doesn't expect us to do all this alone. The word *virtuous* means to be "morally excellent" and "righteous." You may not be perfect on the outside, but when you spend time with the Lord, you will inwardly become virtuous. You don't need to have any righteousness of your own, only what God gives you through Christ (Philippians 3:9). When we freely put on his righteousness, he will guide us daily through every decision we must make, to every person we must help, and to everyone who can help and mentor us.

We do not need to stress about becoming a woman of virtue, checking off lists, and pushing through with our own strength. When we live in Christ, he will beautifully lead us to become the women he wants us to be.

Father, in the name of Jesus, thank you for not requiring me to do anything in my own strength but instead by the power of your Holy Spirit. Craft me into a virtuous and godly woman. Amen.

May I be found in him, freely receiving his righteousness.

DAY 26

The God of Miracles

"Everything is possible for one who believes."
MARK 9:23 NIV

The parting of the Red Sea (Exodus 14). The fall of Jericho (Joshua 6). Daniel in the lion's den (Daniel 6). Water turning into wine (John 2). The Bible records dozens of miracles. Our God is a God who delights in the impossible, during the time of the Bible and still today.

In Matthew 19:26, Jesus declares, "With man this is impossible, but with God all things are possible" (NIV). When the Israelites came to the Red Sea with the Egyptians on their heels, it must have seemed like the end of the road. But God had other plans.

What is your "Red Sea"? Is there something in your life that seems impossible to overcome? In Exodus 14:14, Moses reminds the Israelites—and us today—that "the LORD will fight for you; you need only to be still" (NIV). When you feel weak and powerless, simply rest and call on the Lord. Be still and wait for his voice, trusting that he will do the impossible.

That sounds a lot easier than it actually is, doesn't it? We want to control our own paths. But as children of the Most High, we are invited to release our grip on the limitations of human understanding and believe in God's miraculous intervention. What seems insurmountable to us is an opportunity for God to showcase his unlimited power and glory. While this may be difficult at first, when we pray and ask God to do the impossible, it is like letting go of a huge weight we have been carrying. We don't have to fight every uphill battle alone. We just have to trust God.

This isn't to say that all our prayers will be answered with miracles every time. God has a plan for us, but it doesn't always follow our plans for our lives. Sometimes we will pray for a miracle, but the answer will be no. But when you receive a no from God, don't just resort to weak, faithless prayers to protect your heart from disappointment. Such prayers are directed by fear and cynicism. Continue to pray bold prayers, expecting God to do the impossible. In Jeremiah 32:27, God declares, "Behold, I am the Lord, the God of all flesh. Is anything too hard for me?" (ESV).

Praying boldly is not an exercise in wishful thinking but a declaration of faith. It involves believing that God is not only able but also willing to respond to your petitions in his own time. Your prayers are an expression of faith and a representation of your confidence in God's promises.

When we pray boldly, we open our hearts to God's miraculous possibilities. When God says no to our prayer, don't run away from him. Instead, draw closer to him so he can show you why he said no. When the time is right, he may reveal his glorious plan in a way you hadn't even considered. His ways are better and higher than ours. We must make our requests known with faith and be assured that all things will work together for those he loves and calls according to his purpose (Romans 8:28).

Don't let your doubt and disbelief cloud your trust in Christ. Today's verse reminds us that all we need to do to see God's miracles is to believe. Even faith the size of a mustard seed will move mountains (Matthew 17:20). Let's confront doubt with unwavering belief and bold prayers. Stand strong and face your challenges head-on, knowing that God will reveal his glory through the extraordinary.

Father, refresh my belief in your miracles. I know that you are still working wonders in the lives of your children today, and I want to see and be a part of your miraculous work. Amen.

I know that the God who performed miracles of old is the same God ready to unleash the impossible in my life.

DAY 27

Helicopter Faith

He was also a mighty man in valour,
but he was a leper.
2 KINGS 5:1 KJV

When my son was four years old, all he wanted for Christmas was a remote-controlled helicopter. My husband and I were so excited to share in his joy, eagerly purchasing it, wrapping it with a big bow, and setting it under the tree to wait for Christmas morning. Once Christmas finally arrived, my son could hardly sit through our pre-gift-giving devotional and prayer time. As soon as we uttered "amen," he dove under the tree, tearing open his presents. And there among them was the coveted remote-controlled helicopter.

Of course, he promptly attempted to fly it, only to watch it plummet to the ground. Disappointment clouded his face as he declared, "It's broken." Despite our attempts to reassure him that it was not broken but simply needed batteries, he struggled to understand, deciding that it was useless because it didn't work like he thought it would.

How often do we act like four-year-olds, clinging to our preconceived ideas of how things should unfold? When the outcome doesn't align with your expectations, do you hastily dismiss it as worthless, forgetting to ask God for his divine guidance? Whether it's a career opportunity, a life partner, parenthood, or some other new venture, we mustn't abandon hope when reality diverges from our desires.

Instead, we must ask God to give us peace and understanding in the situation. He has a plan for us, even if we don't understand it. Instead of trying to change God's plan to follow our own, we must pray for his guidance over our lives and follow him even when it doesn't make sense.

In 2 Kings 5:1–13, we find the story of Naaman, a Syrian general with leprosy who journeyed to Jerusalem, seeking Elisha's healing. Since he was wealthy and influential, he expected a personal reception and special treatment. Instead, a messenger directed him to wash seven times in the disgusting waters of the Jordan River. When he was about to give up out of pride and go home, his servants convinced him to at least try washing in the river. And when he did, he was healed.

Naaman nearly missed his blessing because it came

wrapped in a process he didn't expect. In fact, 2 Kings 5:11 tells us what he expected to happen:

> Naaman went away angry and said, "I thought that he would surely come out to me and stand and call on the name of the LORD his God, wave his hand over the spot and cure me of my leprosy." (NIV)

This is the equivalent of my son thinking that he could open his toy helicopter, throw it in the air, and watch it fly without batteries.

After we have communicated our requests to the Lord, we should be ready to accept his response in whatever form it comes and adhere to his guidance. God knows what he is doing. For Naaman, the Lord wanted to deal with two things at the same time: Naaman's healing and his pride. Don't miss out on the Lord because you can't see past your assumptions.

God loves to bring blessings out of difficult circumstances. We can't give up on his miraculous power just because it comes wrapped in a package we don't expect. We must trust the Lord and adhere to his guidance, no matter how strange or difficult it seems.

If you are struggling to let go of your expectations, ask your Christian community for help to hold you accountable. If Naaman had been alone, he never would have listened to God's plan for him, and he would not have received God's blessings. God knows that we need reminders in our faith journey, which is why he created us to help each other. Tell your fellow believers when you are struggling for control. Then come together in prayer.

God knows what he is doing, and he has a great plan for you. Don't miss out on his magnificent blessings just because you don't expect them to come the way they do.

Father, I repent of my need for control. I don't want to miss what you are doing simply because of pride, fear, or expectations. Lord, have your way in my heart. Take over my mind and soul and use them to do your work. In Jesus' name, I pray. Amen.

Lord, I'm getting out of my own way and trusting you all the way.

DAY 28

Reclaiming What Was Lost

He drove out the man; and he placed at the east of the garden of Eden Cherubims, and a flaming sword which turned every way, to keep the way of the tree of life.
GENESIS 3:24 KJV

Imagine receiving an official letter bearing the seal of a mighty king from a powerful nation. The letter declares that you are the long-lost heir to their royal lineage! If you are willing to leave your home and accept your position as heir, great rewards await you. Would you choose to continue living as you do now, or would you embark on a journey to claim your inheritance as a member of the royal family?

When put in earthly terms, it sounds easy. Of course we would set out without hesitation. But the

Bible says that we have received a royal inheritance in God's kingdom. Would you do the same to accept your reward as a member of God's royal family?

Genesis 3 tells the story of two people who forgot that they were a prince and princess of God's family and instead chose to chase after earthly treasures. Adam and Eve were living in perfect communion with God until they forfeited it in exchange for the deceitful promise that they could become like God. God was present with them, walking with them in the garden (Genesis 3:8). He protected them as his son and daughter, and they gave it all up for the fleeting allure of independence. The repercussions of this exchange reverberated through generations, ushering in sin, brokenness, and estrangement from God.

When sin entered the world, Satan began to battle against our identity and worth in God, whispering that we are worthless, forgotten, and inadequate. When you hear this whisper in your ear, shut it out! Cling to God, where your worth truly lies. Galatians 4:7 declares, "You are no longer a slave, but a son, and if a son, then an heir through God" (ESV). Through Christ, we exchange imprisonment and worthlessness for our identity as beloved children and heirs.

Even though Adam and Eve may have forgotten their royal inheritance, God did not. He showed the depth of his love for us in the costly price of redemption that Jesus Christ paid through his sacrifice.

In 2 Corinthians 5:21, we read, "For our sake he made him to be sin who knew no sin, so that in him we might become the righteousness of God" (ESV). Jesus, the sinless Son of God, bore the weight of our sins, offering us a chance to exchange our brokenness for his righteousness. The cost of redemption was immeasurable, emphasizing God's incomprehensible love for his creation.

There is more to Christ's redeeming power. Not only did he reinstate our royal position, but he also looks forward to returning what is ours as we journey through life. Joel 2:25 reads: "I will repay you for the years the locusts have eaten—the great locust and the young locust, the other locusts and the locust swarm—my great army that I sent among you" (NIV). This verse is a promise of restoration from God. God will restore what has been lost or destroyed, whether physically, emotionally, or spiritually. It's a message of hope and assurance that God's grace and mercy can bring renewal and redemption as we walk with him.

Christ's sacrifice had profound implications for humanity, including the reclamation of what was lost through sin. Through Jesus, God declared anew that we are heirs to the kingdom of heaven. We don't have to live in bondage to sin because we have been freed through faith. Cast off Satan's lies of worthlessness and receive your inheritance so that you can live in righteousness, acceptance, and joy.

Our worth is no longer defined by the brokenness of the fall but by the immeasurable love of the one who redeemed us. Take your royal position in Christ and embrace your identity and authority as a child of God through faith in Jesus Christ. Fully receive your spiritual inheritance and position as heir to the kingdom of God.

Jesus has reclaimed what was lost and made a way for us to come back to him. Choose to enjoy the beauty and freedom of his truth.

Father, in the name of Jesus, I am set on fire. I no longer desire for any part of my life to be less than what you have planned. Thank you for my royal inheritance. Because of you, I know that I will walk through this life victoriously. Amen.

I'm overwhelmed by you, Lord. I will live according to my identity as a member of your royal family.

DAY 29

Impacting the Kingdom

Go ye therefore, and teach all nations, baptizing them in the name of the Father, and of the Son, and of the Holy Ghost.

MATTHEW 28:19 KJV

Whenever my mother enters a store, she hands out Daily Bread pamphlets to strangers. Responses vary—some reject the pamphlets, while others are genuinely pleased, even seeking prayer and occasionally offering to cover my mother's grocery expenses. Upon returning home, my mother fervently prays for everyone she encountered that day, hoping that they will either embrace faith in the Lord or deepen their existing relationship with him. This is her method of going out and spreading the good news.

Jesus calls all of us to share the good news of his gospel. Today's verse is called the Great Commission. It is God's call for intentional action, his instruction that we step outside our comfort zones and share the gospel with people from all walks of life, making disciples and baptizing people. Ask yourself, *Am I doing this? And if not, why?* Are you willing to fulfill Jesus' request with obedience and honor?

Fulfilling the Great Commission is not just about sharing the gospel, though that is part of it. Jesus did not just share the gospel and then leave; he connected with people and made disciples, developing relationships with them. God calls us to do the same. We must share life, build community, impart spiritual truths, and model the transformative power of a life surrendered to the Lord. It doesn't matter where you are. The unreached are ready to know that there is a God who loves them and created them for a beautiful purpose.

But how do we do this? One of the reasons many believers are hesitant to share the gospel is because they do not feel equipped to do so effectively. If you're struggling to know how to disciple believers, here are a few steps to get you started.

First, you must understand the people you want to disciple. In Acts 17:22–23, Paul engaged with the Athenians by learning about their culture. When you take the time to get to know people, you will understand where they come from and why they believe what they do. This information will then show you how to minister to them. This approach does not just apply when speaking to people from other countries either. God created every single one of us differently. Learn about the people near you, whether at work, school, church, or even your local gym or coffee shop.

Second, teaching others to observe all that Jesus commanded requires biblical knowledge and practical wisdom. Once you know people's needs, turn to the Bible for God's truth. Memorize Scripture passages that you can share with others on the spot or practice telling your own story by using Bible verses from your daily study. We can only teach others after we have learned the truth ourselves. When you immerse yourself in Scripture daily, God's truth will naturally pour out of you.

Finally, prayer is a powerful catalyst for fulfilling the Great Commission. In Ephesians 6:19, Paul requested prayer for boldness in proclaiming the gospel. Pray boldly that God will open doors and empower you through the Holy Spirit. Prayer is the heartbeat of effective and impactful mission endeavors. Prayer tells the Lord that you don't want to fulfill his commission with your own strength and ideas; you desire guidance from him. God is waiting for you to ask him for help, and he will give you strength.

Let's embrace the Great Commission with joy and see it as a personal responsibility. Every believer is called to share God's love for the world and make disciples for his kingdom.

Father, I pray that you give me the boldness to honor your request to fulfill the Great Commission. Lead the way, Lord. May I become a vessel of hope, love, and salvation for the people you have placed around me today. Amen.

Wherever you lead, I'll go; I'll follow my Christ who loves me so.

DAY 30

The Power of Fasting

Is not this the fast that I have chosen? to loose the bands of wickedness, to undo the heavy burdens, and to let the oppressed go free, and that ye break every yoke?
ISAIAH 58:6 KJV

Fasting has long been a common practice within the church, but over time, the practice has changed. While many still fast by completely avoiding food, some take a different approach by deleting social media or ridding themselves of other indulgences for a time.

But fasting goes beyond mere abstention from something; it calls for a genuine pursuit of God's presence. I've fasted many times throughout my life, but rarely was my focus and approach aligned with the true essence of fasting. I must admit that in the past, I sometimes looked for ways to bypass the sacrifice, such as resorting to sugar-free snacks when fasting from sugar to avoid the discomfort of going without sweets. My heart wasn't completely centered on the sacrifice.

However, as I've matured in the Lord, my perspective has evolved. I now try to prioritize not only abstaining from pleasurable indulgences but also from substitutes, with a focus on deepening my intimacy with the Lord.

When we understand the meaning of fasting, it will act as a spiritual weapon against the forces that seek to keep us captive. Today's verse tells us that fasting has the power to destroy Satan's strongholds and break any chains that bind us. Fasting breaks our reliance on earthly distractions so we can instead declare dependence on God's strength to break the chains of sin, addiction, and oppression. We are then positioned to experience Christ's freedom. When we accept this freedom, God will begin to make breakthroughs in our life and miraculously intervene in our battles against sin.

One of Satan's most prominent tools in today's world is distraction. Messages blare at us from everywhere, and it's hard to hear God's voice within all that noise. Fasting pulls us out of the commotion, clearing our perspective and enhancing our sensitivity to God's voice. In Acts 13:2, we see the early church fasting and seeking the Lord's guidance: "While they were worshiping the Lord and fasting, the Holy Spirit said, 'Set apart for me Barnabas and Saul for the work to which I have called them'" (NIV). Their fast gave them the right mindset to hear God's direction. Like the early believers, set aside your earthly pleasures to receive clarity and revelation.

Fasting is also an act of humility before the Lord. In Psalm 35:13, David declared, "When they were ill, I put on sackcloth and humbled myself with fasting" (NIV). Fasting expresses our humility toward God by weakening our flesh and strengthening our spirit. It is an intentional posture of surrender that expresses our need for divine intervention. When we seek God with a contrite heart rather than focusing on earthly things, our intimacy with God deepens, and he aligns our heart with his will.

In Luke 4:1–2, Jesus, filled with the Holy Spirit, fasted for forty days in preparation for his ministry ahead. When we fast, we tell God that we are ready for him to mold us into vessels ready to fulfill his plan. We open our hearts and minds to him, bowing down before his glorious power.

While discussing fasting, Isaiah 58:11 tells us that "the Lord will guide you continually, and satisfy your soul in drought, and strengthen your bones" (NKJV). This is one of the most amazing things about fasting. After we go to God in fasting and prayer, we will discover the truth of this verse. As we sacrifice, he guides us, satisfies our souls, and strengthens us. The next time you fast, enter into it with a mindset of holiness and sacrifice, understanding that God will provide everything you need.

Father, in the name of Jesus, I thank you for the opportunity to express my total dependence on you. You are my everything, and I surrender all to you, my King. Thank you for leading me through a time of fasting that propels me into deeper intimacy with you. Amen.

I will fast to receive a spiritual breakthrough in my life.

DAY 31

Waiting Faithfully

As for you, ye thought evil against me;
but God meant it unto good.
Genesis 50:20 KJV

Disappointment and pain are never enjoyable, and they're challenging to overcome. But these moments unveil truth. In the midst of adversity, you will be able to discern the authenticity of your relationship with Jesus Christ. In the Scriptures, Joseph stands out as a prime example of someone who displayed exceptional godly character and integrity despite horrifying challenges.

When the Israelites received a new king, a priest would anoint him, usually by pouring oil on his head. This was to signify that God had chosen this man to be the leader of the Lord's people. Joseph may not have been a king, but he was anointed by God as surely as David or Solomon.

The word *anoint* comes from the Hebrew word *mashach*, which means "to consecrate."[4] This refers not just to kingship but also to any specific purpose that God has given to someone. When a person is anointed, they receive God's power to fulfill that purpose. Without God's approval, presence, and power, Joseph would not have survived the challenges of his life and still arrived at his God-appointed destination.

One of the most important things to remember about anointing is that it is not about us but about God. When he anoints us, it means that we receive his blessing on our lives, and he will use us to accomplish his will. Anointing is a sign of his approval, which all believers should desire.

But how do we tell if God has anointed us while trials and tribulations surround us? Extended periods of waiting can be arduous, yet the Joseph anointing teaches us to place our trust in God's timing and process. Joseph was sold into slavery; he was wrongfully accused and thrown into prison. Yet through all that, he simply listened for God and did the best he could right where he was. Be like Joseph and trust that God's power is at work. Listen for his voice and hear his words.

Genesis 39:23 says, "The keeper of the prison paid no attention to anything that was in Joseph's charge, because the LORD was with him. And whatever he did,

---

4 Strong, *Strong's Expanded Exhaustive Concordance of the Bible*, H4886.

the Lord made it succeed" (ESV). Joseph committed to integrity even in the face of adversity. In today's world, where moral compromises abound, the Joseph anointing calls us to stand firm in our commitment to righteousness, no matter what.

When we face challenges, some people will hurt us rather than help us. Satan has humanity in his clutches, and we will face his horrific power again and again, often through the people around us. Part of remaining faithful to God and trusting in his power is trusting him to judge his own people. It is not our job to judge but to forgive. Forgiveness is the path to freedom.

Joseph's ability to forgive, even after years of betrayal, is a testament to the transformative power of grace. In today's verse, he forgave his brothers, who had sold him into slavery, and he recognized that it was all part of God's plan. That couldn't have been easy! But when the Holy Spirit empowers us, we can do anything. The Joseph anointing calls us to extend grace because we recognize that God can use even the darkest circumstances for our good and his glory.

Whatever you face, remain faithful. When you face challenges, remain faithful. When you are blessed, remain faithful. Everything is God's plan. Stay humble, grateful, generous, and loving. Be kind to those who support you and to those who are against you. The Lord's anointing is on you. Just like God did for Joseph, he has raised you to a place of influence for a great purpose designed to bring souls into the kingdom for his glory.

Father, I thank you for the example of Joseph's life marked by integrity, patience, forgiveness, and unwavering faith in your redemptive plan. I thank you for your hand of favor and approval upon my life so that I may bring you glory. Amen.

If the Lord were not on my side, where would I be? He is my everything.

DAY 32

Radiating Love in the Church

"Love your neighbor as yourself."
MATTHEW 22:39 NIV

As Jesus approached the conclusion of his earthly life, he offered a prayer for unity among believers, expressing his desire for them to be as united as he and the Father are (John 17:20–23). We as a church have not been practicing this unity very well recently.

In 1960, Martin Luther King Jr. observed that Sundays in America are the most segregated time of the week.[5] This is still true today. Recent research

5 Martin Luther King, Jr., "The Most Segregated Hour in America," *Meet the Press* interview, April 17, 1960, posted April 29, 2014 by Jason Tripp, https://www.youtube.com.

highlights the ongoing struggle to achieve diversity and unity within the body of believers.[6]

There is diversity in everything God created. Every organism or object serves a different purpose, and each is necessary to bring life and beauty to the world. Consider, for instance, the human body. Our bodies are made up of many different types of cells, each with distinct functions, but they all work toward a common purpose: sustaining life. The body of Christ is the same. Each believer is completely different, with different strengths and weaknesses. We must rely on one another to fulfill God's intended purpose, remaining united while bringing our unique gifts, contributions, and challenges to the table. These differences are designed to foster growth and unity within the body of believers.

In today's verse, Jesus commands us to love our neighbors as much as we love ourselves. Besides loving God, Jesus told us this was his most important command, which means that it should form the bedrock of our Christian identity. We are meant to reflect the love of Christ in all our relationships, transcending personal differences and respecting each other.

This command emphasizes the selfless, sacrificial, and unconditional nature of love that God calls Christians to demonstrate toward one another. It's not just about showing affection or kindness but also about

6 Ryan P. Burge, "50 Years after MLK, Sunday Segregation Isn't Theological," *Christianity Today* (website), April 4, 2018, https://www.christianitytoday.com.

embodying the same kind of sacrificial love that Christ demonstrated through his life, death, and resurrection. It is not always easy to find common ground, but love finds a way to bring us together and connect us under one God.

Paul addressed this issue as well: "As for the one who is weak in faith, welcome him, but not to quarrel over opinions" (Romans 14:1 ESV). We are called to love and welcome others, but we are human. When we don't invite God into every relationship, our differences will spawn enmity and misunderstanding, even among the church.

In 1 Corinthians 12:4–6, Paul wrote, "There are different gifts, but the same Spirit. There are different ministries, but the same Lord. And there are different activities, but the same God works all of them in each person" (CSB). When God created us, he intentionally gave each of us different gifts and passions. We each are uniquely made for what God has appointed us to do, from teaching to leading to administrating. Though we have been appointed to different callings and positions, we have all been anointed for one purpose: the advancement of the kingdom of God.

To grow a vibrant garden filled with colorful flowers, fruits, and herbs, a gardener must prune any unhealthy branches. In the same way, for our beautiful, diverse church to flourish, we must prune unhealthy branches of dissension with our shears of love and grace. Rather than shying away from moments of misunderstanding and discontent, we should approach them with open hearts, attentively listening and fervently praying. Through this process, we can cultivate a safe environment conducive to learning and growth, discipling each other as a church to better share God's love with a watching world.

Approach your neighbors with humility and empathy. They will be different from you, for God intentionally created them that way. Remember that he loves them deeply just as he loves you. He deliberately created each of us with unique talents and abilities so that we may celebrate one another as we use these gifts to express our love for the Lord. We must never compare gifts or look down on others for their differences. Let us celebrate our individuality as children of Christ with hearts filled with love for each other as Christ loves us.

Father, help me to see everyone as your children rather than just seeing our differences. I desire to embrace our differences wholeheartedly and to understand that you created us this way. Lord, I reject any resentment or anger I may have toward the people around me. In Jesus' name. Amen.

May my actions bring you joy as I step outside of my comfort zone to extend love and unity to the people around me.

DAY 33

Unleashing the Royal Roar

Speak up for those who cannot speak for themselves,
ensure justice for those being crushed.
PROVERBS 31:8 NLT

Why does the Enemy work so hard to silence our voices? What tools does he use to do this? Has he silenced your voice? These questions explore the profound importance of using your voice—a royal roar—to bring transformative change to your family, communities, and nation. As believers, our voices must be committed to justice, righteousness, and the pursuit of God's purposes.

The Enemy knows the power of a believer's voice. When a believer raises their voice to speak life, hope, and love to what looks dead and hopeless, God's life will dispel the darkness surrounding them. Proverbs 18:21 tells us that "death and life are in the power of the tongue" (ESV). When we boldly raise our voices in God's truth and authority, we will defeat the Enemy and tear down his tools.

Keep an eye out for the tools the Enemy uses to silence believers, such as self-hatred, fear, depression, shame, and timidity. When we do not keep our eyes trained on God, we allow these tactics to creep into our lives. Stand strong in the Lord and battle the Enemy's schemes with prayer.

God raised Esther into a time of terrible judgment on the Jewish people. Esther's voice, initially silenced by fear, resonated as a powerful force for change after she turned to God for guidance. In Esther 4:14, her cousin Mordecai's words challenged her: "Who knows whether you have not come to the kingdom for such a time as this?" (ESV). Esther courageously took the risk and spoke up. As a result, an entire nation, the nation from which Christ would be born, was saved from total annihilation.

Your voice has great power as you proclaim God's Word on the earth. Your voice holds the potential to speak life, truth, and transformation to all the world. We can either use this power to spread lies or to speak truth. Esther recognized this power and, with courage, used her voice to alter the course of a nation. Just like

Esther, your voice can bring life, challenge injustice, and inspire real and lasting change.

Esther's initial hesitation is understandable; fear can shroud our voices. But as believers, we are called to break the chains of silence and speak up for righteousness. Proverbs 31:8–9 challenges us to "speak up for those who cannot speak for themselves; ensure justice for those being crushed. Yes, speak up for the poor and helpless, and see that they get justice" (NLT). God has entrusted us with a voice not only for personal expression but also to advocate for those who cannot speak for themselves.

We have the sacred responsibility to use our voices to ensure that justice, mercy, and righteousness prevail. Your voice can be a catalyst that unlocks transformation. Your courage and willingness to risk everything for a righteous cause will dismantle Satan's wicked plans. Your voice, aligned with the principles of God's kingdom, has the power to shift beliefs, break chains, and bring about divine transformation—the Enemy's worst nightmare.

You may encounter resistance, uncertainties, or even persecution, but your assurance lies in trusting God's providence. Esther's trust in God's sovereignty propelled her to speak boldly. Likewise, as you raise your royal roar for justice and righteousness, trust that God is orchestrating the outcome. When you use your voice, you will inspire and empower others to do the same.

Father, in the name of Jesus, I am ready to embrace the transformative power of using my voice—a royal roar echoing justice, righteousness, and God's purposes. Esther's courageous voice altered the course of a nation, and likewise, my voice holds the potential to impact the world around me. As I speak life, truth, and justice, my voice resonates with the heart of God, bringing about transformative change for such a time as this. Amen.

I have the power to change my life, family, community, nation, and world. I just have to open my mouth and use my voice as the Holy Spirit leads.

DAY 34

The Cost of Compassion

"Greater love has no one than this,
that someone lay down his life for his friends."
JOHN 15:13 ESV

When I was a teenager, I visited El Salvador to do mission work with my father. One of the families we helped lived in the poorest conditions—eight people sharing a two-room house without running water. When we visited them, they offered us a huge basket of fruits and vegetables. Obviously, they needed it more than we did, but it was their cultural custom to honor guests with their best gift, and they were excited to do so. It pained me to accept their gift, but refusing it would have been disrespectful. Ultimately, they cared more about generosity, hospitality, and gratitude than their own physical well-being.

I couldn't stop thinking about their boundless compassion. Despite having far less than I did, they were willing to give more than I had ever given. Their selflessness illuminated my selfishness and earthly desires. I kept the best for myself when I should have been giving sacrificially.

In Luke 10:33–34, the Samaritan gave of his time and money to care for a complete stranger from an enemy nation. He "bound up his wounds, pouring on oil and wine. Then he set him on his own animal and brought him to an inn and took care of him" (ESV). The Samaritan in this story showed genuine compassion, putting his neighbor above everything else. This sort of compassion is expected of all Christians.

In Philippians 2:3–4, Paul said to "do nothing from selfish ambition or conceit, but in humility count others more significant than yourselves. Let each of you look not only to his own interests, but also to the interests of others" (ESV). To take on God's compassion, we must ask him to remove our human selfishness. It's a deliberate shift from a me-centered mindset to a Christ-centered one. Instead of actively looking for ways to make ourselves happier, we must actively consider how we can help the people around us.

Contemporary culture encourages everything that God's compassion does not. Instead of giving sacrificially and putting others first, the world says to fight for status and personal gain. But as Christians, we know the truth in Matthew 6:19–21:

> "Do not store up for yourselves treasures on earth, where moths and vermin destroy, and where thieves break in and steal. But store up for yourselves treasures in heaven, where moths and vermin do not destroy, and where thieves do not break in and steal. For where your treasure is, there your heart will be also." (NIV)

Hoarding earthly wealth will only breed resentment and greed. Anything we receive here on earth is a gift from God, and we are meant to steward it as such. Instead of reveling in earthly treasures, share in God's compassion and store up in heaven treasures of love, joy, and peace. These will last forever.

If you are ever struggling to live like the Good Samaritan did, remember that we have the ultimate example of compassion right before us: our Savior Jesus. In John 15:13, Jesus declared, "Greater love has no one than this, that someone lay down his life for his friends" (ESV). Jesus broke the power of hell, death, and the grave through the power of his sacrifice. He is well acquainted with the power released when we give, love, and serve from a place of sacrifice.

When we willingly shoulder the cost of sacrifice, Christ's love will radiate brightly, ignite a ripple effect of compassion and unity, and foster a healthy, God-led sacrificial love within the church.

Father, teach me to give sacrificially without fear of want. May I be like you, compassionate and merciful to all your beloved children. Amen.

All that I have is yours, so I gladly offer it up to you. Freely you have given, so freely I give.

DAY 35

Joy in Generosity

Every good gift and every perfect gift is from above.
JAMES 1:17 ESV

During my senior year of high school, I joined a group of young women on a trip to El Salvador to serve people in need. Upon our return to the United States, a local church asked us to share our experiences. As I sat in the audience and listened to the young women speak, I couldn't help but notice how guilty they seemed to feel. They all voiced feelings of shame about the luxuries they enjoyed in the United States. I thought to myself, *Would God want us to serve those in need only to be burdened with guilt and shame afterward?* I didn't believe so.

When it was my turn to take the stage, I shared a different perspective. I told the audience that I had found the rich in spirit among the poor and, at times, the poor in spirit among the rich. I learned so much from the Salvadorian people and their principles, principles that I continue to follow and will follow for the rest of my life. Yes, these people were devastatingly poor in their physical needs, but they were also far wealthier in other ways that we could not begin to understand.

I explained to the audience that while I was aware of my abundant blessings and profoundly grateful for them, I felt no guilt. I knew the Lord would bless these beautiful people either through our hands or the hands of another.

Feeling guilty or apologizing for our blessings, whether it is where we live or what we have, stems from a sense of unworthiness. We feel guilty for enjoying certain freedoms and possessions because we consider this enjoyment selfish or prideful. But the blessings themselves are neither selfish nor prideful. They are not meant to evoke condemnation but rather to extend an invitation to dwell in the abundance of his grace.

Romans 8:1 provides assurance to believers, saying, "There is therefore now no condemnation for those who are in Christ Jesus" (ESV). And whether we consider ourselves worthy is ultimately irrelevant, for we never will be. We must recognize our unworthiness, thank God for his goodness and boundless generosity, and then set that guilt aside.

Feeling guilty is not a noble display of humility either. True humility comes when we stop allowing our external circumstances, whatever they may be, to dictate our value and worth, as only Christ fulfills these in our hearts. Instead, we must see blessings as a loan from God. We should enjoy them when we can, and when God calls us to give them away, we must thank him for the loan and give them up gladly.

God further calls those who are blessed with much to give to those with little. We witness breakthroughs like never before when we share our blessings. I've seen God work through me and through others to help those who are less fortunate to break free of the chains of generational poverty. In helping to provide resources for education and funding to create jobs, we share our blessings and acknowledge God as the ultimate source of all good things.

I personally consider it a privilege to play a part in God's answer to their prayers and an even greater privilege to witness their growing prosperity on earth and in heaven. Their pure joy at simply being able to provide for their families and communities is breathtaking.

Some people struggle to survive, while others have more than they could ever use. We live in a fallen world, and until Jesus returns, this disparity will always be a problem because of Satan and sin. God's answer to this problem is the church. James 1:17 serves as a reminder for believers: "Every good gift and every perfect gift is from above, coming down from the

Father of lights, with whom there is no variation or shadow due to change" (ESV).

Our blessings are gifts that our loving Father bestows upon us, and we are to treat them as such. Instead of feeling guilty, we can be joyful that we have the resources to help God's people. When we embrace this joy, we're able to better comprehend his delight in blessing his children.

Rejoice in your gifts, share them with others, and help those in need by sharing your blessings with thankfulness and joy. They will become a testament to the forgiveness and redemption we find in Christ.

Father, thank you for the countless blessings you have bestowed upon me. I will forever praise you for all you've done for me. Please help me to be a blessing to others and to give generously as you direct me. Amen.

You are a good Father who finds joy in blessing your children.

DAY 36

Gossip in Disguise

Let no corrupt communication proceed out of your mouth, but that which is good to the use of edifying.
EPHESIANS 4:29 KJV

The Bible warns against gossip again and again. In today's verse, Paul strictly forbade it, saying that it is not edifying. But it's hard. Try as we may to avoid gossip, even the most well-meaning people sometimes fall into its trap. Have you ever been privy to tantalizing information that you just couldn't help but share? I know I certainly have. I have felt terrible after leaving a lunch with a friend or ending a call and realizing that I had entertained gossip without even noticing it.

Gossiping should not be a part of a believer's lifestyle. In fact, Proverbs 16:28 says, "A perverse person stirs up conflict, and a gossip separates close friends" (NIV). We might justify gossip by trusting that the person we've confided in won't spread the information further, but this is gossip in disguise. In order to be a good steward of our relationships, we first must examine our motivations. Are we genuinely praying for this person and expressing deep care and concern for them, or are we driven more by the desire to be the first to share the news?

We must also watch our conversations and keep them free from harmful words toward each other. Gossip is subtle. When we don't guard against it, it will infiltrate our conversations disguised as care, concern, or prayer requests. Gossip can be sneaky by luring us into a conversation that doesn't reflect the heart of God. Staying sensitive toward the Holy Spirit helps us to recognize the weight of our words and guard our heart before gossip threatens to ruin our relationships.

Gossip is so dangerous because it doesn't look threatening at first. Proverbs 26:22 describes it vividly: "The words of a whisperer are like delicious morsels; they go down into the inner parts of the body" (ESV). Gossip can be appealing, like delicious morsels. When someone shares a secret with you, it may not seem harmful to tell it to just one other person. It's easy to think that someone will never know if you talk about them behind their back.

However, these things leak out. Once you've begun to spread information, you have no way to stop it. It will go beyond the surface and penetrate the inner parts of our heart, destroying our relationships and damaging what may not be immediately visible.

The book of Proverbs offers more advice. Proverbs 4:23 tells us: "Keep your heart with all vigilance, for from it flow the springs of life" (ESV). Proverbs 11:13 says, "Whoever goes about slandering reveals secrets, but he who is trustworthy in spirit keeps a thing covered" (ESV). Or check out Proverbs 26:20, which says, "For lack of wood the fire goes out, and where there is no whisperer, quarreling ceases" (ESV).

When we care about others, we will speak the truth in love and actively monitor our conversations, ensuring that our words align with the principles of love, grace, and edification. Take Psalm 19:14 to heart, which says, "Let the words of my mouth and the meditation of my heart be acceptable in your sight, O LORD, my rock and my redeemer" (ESV). Reject gossip, slander, and misinformation. These are tools that breed dissension and resentment for our brothers and sisters in Christ.

Am I my brother and sister's keeper? To this question I offer a resounding yes. We should protect each other and vow not to harm the family of God with our words. In fact, it should bring us great joy to honor each other by refusing to entertain gossip. Jesus taught his followers to treat others as they would like to be treated. Engaging in gossip violates this rule.

As we guard our hearts, may our words reflect the

transformative power of Christ's love, bringing life and grace to those around us.

Father, I submit myself to you and repent for every moment that I've participated in gossip. I want to speak words of life over myself, my loved ones, and my friends. May I find no pleasure in the downfall of others but earnestly pray as you would direct. Amen.

I shall allow only life to spring forth from my lips.

DAY 37

A Time of Breakthrough

"I sought for a man among them, that should make up the hedge, and stand in the gap before me for the land, that I should not destroy it."
EZEKIEL 22:30 KJV

Every morning, as the first light breaks through the windows, my mother rises to pray. She begins by opening her hymn book and singing praises to the Lord before diving into her devotional, praying and interceding for her loved ones. One Christmas, she made an unusual request: a large map and globe. I couldn't help but question the gift, as it seemed an odd request. Yet she insisted, so I complied.

Little did I know her intention: to spread the map across her wall and use it as a visual aid for her prayers for the nations of the world. With her hand laid on the map and globe, she prayed fervently for each region's people, governments, and Christian ministries.

Her unwavering commitment to global intercession left me awestruck. I couldn't help but admire her dedication. I want to call in breakthroughs and seek God's transformative intervention because of my mom's example of deep and committed intercession. It's encouraging to know that somewhere another believer like my mom is compelled by the Holy Spirit to pray for me. Isn't it amazing that someone you may never meet is praying for you, your family, and your nation? The love of God overwhelms me at times when I think of his goodness and his extreme provision for us.

Mark 11:24 assures believers of the power of faith-filled prayers: "I tell you, whatever you ask in prayer, believe that you have received it, and it will be yours" (ESV). Relentless intercession requires an unwavering belief that God hears and responds to the cries of his children, as well as a tenacious faith that stands firm in the face of challenges. Whether my mom has a great day or a frustrating day, she never lets it affect her commitment to pray. To her, it is not an emotionally-led option but a spiritual duty to remain consistent in prayer. Lives depend on my mom's prayer, and she finds pleasure in partnering with God to uplift his children around the world.

Today's verse explains the partnership between God and intercessors on the earth. God seeks those who will build up the protective wall through prayer, preventing destruction. He doesn't want his creation to fall into sin, and he wants us to be the ones to urge people into his glorious love and light. But in the context of today's verse, no one was willing to pray for the world. When we aren't willing to share God's light with the people around us, Satan's hold on our world will only grow stronger.

Ephesians 6:12 says, "Our struggle is not against flesh and blood, but against the rulers, against the authorities, against the powers of this dark world and against the spiritual forces of evil in the heavenly realms" (NIV). Intercessors battle in these realms, calling for God's power to bind the darkness and setting the stage for God's miracles, signs, and wonders.

Intercession is one of our most powerful tools to destroy the works of the Enemy. You don't need to go anywhere or do anything except pray with faith, trusting in the Lord. You can send prayers from your bedroom, your desk, your car. Constantly do battle against the spiritual darkness spread across this earth. You may never know the full impact of your prayers, but God does. Be the one who prays for breakthroughs and intercedes for others to fill the gaps between our sinfulness and God's glory.

God is looking to see whom he can partner with to release his will on the earth. Can he count on you to commit to intercession so the world can experience the passion and wonder of his love?

Father I ask for a heart that is committed to daily intercession. I long to partner with you to see true and lasting breakthroughs spread throughout the earth. Please give me the power to stand in the gap for those who do not know you. And thank you for those whom you lead to pray for me. I love you, Lord, and I know you hold this world in your hands. Amen.

The prayers of the righteous bring redemption and glory.

DAY 38

A Heart of Perseverance

Continue earnestly in prayer,
being vigilant in it with thanksgiving.
COLOSSIANS 4:2 NKJV

I once read a joke online that said, "I tried to throw in the towel, but God threw it back and said, 'Now wipe your face. You're almost there.'" We can't give up. Regardless of what we are facing, we simply cannot throw in the towel. Galatians 6:9 encourages believers with a message of perseverance: "Let us not grow weary of doing good, for in due season we will reap, if we do not give up" (ESV). Calling in breakthroughs involves an enduring commitment to seeking God's intervention, even in the face of delays or apparent challenges. Our due season of reaping the goodness of God will come as we persist in prayer.

In Luke 18:2–5, Jesus tells his disciples a parable to explain the importance of perseverance:

> In a certain town, there was a judge who neither feared God nor respected other people. There was also in that town a widow who kept coming to him and saying, "Give me a judgment against the man who is trying to ruin me." For a long time he refused; but after awhile, he said to himself, "I don't fear God, and I don't respect other people; but because this widow is such a nudnik, I will see to it that she gets justice—otherwise, she'll keep coming and pestering me till she wears me out!" (CJB)

In verses 7–8, Jesus goes on to point out, "Won't God grant justice to his chosen people who cry out to him day and night? Is he delaying long over them? I tell you that he will judge in their favor, and quickly!" (CJB). If you are waiting on the Lord, do not stop crying out to him. We don't know God's timing. Your answer might be just around the corner.

God likes to display his glory through answered prayers, so don't give up. Expect that God will either do what you've asked or do something else even greater. His ways are superior to ours, so our trust and expectations are safe in him. He will always do what is best by making all things work together for those who love him and are called according to his purpose (Romans 8:28).

When I am struggling to persevere in prayer, I will write down my prayers and put dates next to them. This way, I can look back and remember when God answered my prayers and what his answer was. It's good to look at past answers you have received so you can eagerly anticipate the answers to come.

Today's verse reminds us to stay vigilant in prayer. Look back at what God has done for you in the past to see how he will prepare a way for you in the future. We cannot always see the good things God does, but we know that they are there and that he is working. All throughout the Bible are stories of God working in ways unknown to people. Even Jesus' death was horrible and tragic for his friends—until he rose again to save us.

In Luke 11:5–10, Jesus encourages his followers to ask, seek, and knock persistently in prayer, assuring them that God will respond. This persistence in prayer is not about manipulating God or wearing him down but rather about demonstrating trust, faith, and dependence on God's provision and timing. The verbs *ask*, *seek*, and *knock* suggest a progression of intensity and commitment in prayer. Asking involves making requests known to God, seeking implies actively searching for his will, and knocking suggests persistently striving for entrance into God's holy presence.

Jesus emphasizes that everyone who asks receives, everyone who seeks finds, and to everyone who knocks, the door will be opened. God is attentive to his children's prayers. He will respond according to his perfect wisdom and timing. Our job is to believe that, at the appointed time, God will do what is best for our lives.

We have no concept of all that God is accomplishing through our persistent prayers. All we see is what is right in front of us, but God sees the big picture. He knows what's best for us, and he is working all things together for our good. Pray with perseverance and keep going, for we do not know God's time and plan.

Father, in the name of Jesus, I am grateful that you hear my prayers and, with great joy, are preparing to answer them in your timing. You reveal your love for me through these answers. Please help me to persevere through my trials constantly. I love you. In Jesus' name. Amen.

With the Lord by my side, I have everything I need to withstand the darkest night. Morning is coming.

DAY 39

Transformative Worship

Enter into his gates with thanksgiving,
and into his courts with praise.
PSALM 100:4 KJV

I adore worshiping through song. It allows me to harness my passion for music and singing as I offer up expressions of gratitude to honor my Creator. He deserves every ounce of praise and adoration we can offer him.

Worship became a lifeline for me during one of the darkest seasons of my life. When I lost yet another pregnancy, I was devastated. I didn't know what to do or where to turn. But that was when I realized that I needed to fix my gaze on the Lord to weather the storm threatening to engulf me. As I began to worship, I felt his love like a protective shield, deflecting the Enemy's arrows, arrows designed to convince me that God wasn't good and that I should blame him for my loss.

The Enemy exploited my grief and anguish, sowing seeds of doubt and lies and hoping to drive a wedge between me and my loving heavenly Father. He weaseled into my mind and hammered me with questions like, *Why would God allow me to experience this pain?* This was a twisted lie that the Enemy hoped I would buy. But the thought didn't feel right in my spirit.

Once I recognized the devil's deception, I repented and asked the Lord to escort me through this difficult time like only he could. When I worshiped, I felt the Lord surround me with his healing love and guide me through my sorrow. My heart was overwhelmed, but God's comfort was sweet. In my most painful moments, my relationship with the Lord grew.

In John 4:23, Jesus speaks to the Samaritan woman about worship: "The hour is coming, and is now here, when the true worshipers will worship the Father in spirit and truth, for the Father is seeking such people to worship him" (ESV). True worship involves a heart connection with God. It goes beyond a mere ritual or a love of song and music; it's an intimate encounter where believers seek God in authenticity and sincerity. Whether we are experiencing peace or troubles, worship is a powerful weapon that plants our focus on God, the source of life, peace, and power.

Today's verse encourages believers to enter God's presence with thanksgiving and praise. When you come before God, come with a heart that acknowledges God's goodness and overflows with boundless love for him.

Romans 12:1 tells us what the meaning of worship truly is: "I appeal to you therefore, brothers, by the mercies of God, to present your bodies as a living sacrifice, holy and acceptable to God, which is your spiritual worship" (ESV). Worship isn't just singing; it is anything we do that brings honor to God and shows our adoration for his glory. It is surrendering our lives and presenting ourselves as living sacrifices to God's ministry. We can worship through giving, serving, and obeying him even when it is hard. All these things are a form of worship. We must allow God to work in and through our lives for his glory through every circumstance.

Revelation 4:11 gives us insight into what worship sounds like as we express God's worth: "You are worthy, our Lord and God, to receive glory and honor and power, for you created all things, and by your will they were created and have their being" (NIV). Psalm 29:2 also says, "Ascribe to the LORD the glory due his name; worship the LORD in the splendor of his holiness" (NIV). Worshiping the Lord is beautiful and blesses you just as much as it blesses him.

May we all approach worship with a spirit of authenticity, gratitude, and surrender, knowing that in the presence of God, we are being transformed. God is everything we need. He is the great and mighty

Creator, the savior of all the universe. We must offer up our lives in worship to him every day. As we mature in the knowledge of God through worship, may our lives become a fragrant offering, reflecting the glory of the One we worship.

Father, in the name of Jesus, I thank you for the opportunity to worship your holy name. With joy, I receive your invitation to come into your presence and enjoy the profound journey that deepens my relationship with you, shapes hearts with gratitude, and transforms lives into the likeness of Christ. Amen.

Worshiping the Lord during ferocious storms will save me from drowning.

DAY 40

Longing for God's Face

When Simon saw that the Spirit was given at the laying on of the apostles' hands, he offered them money.
ACTS 8:18 NIV

While volunteering at a shelter during the holidays, I chatted with a man who had been living there for about a week. Roughly ten minutes into our discussion, I asked whether he had ever contemplated surrendering his life to Jesus. He shared that he had become a Christian in the past because he believed that God would bring him wealth. When this didn't happen, he abandoned his faith.

His words lingered in my mind for days, prompting me to reflect on my own expectations and perceptions of God. When you find yourself disappointed in your walk with God, ask yourself why you follow Jesus. What are your desires and aspirations? Are they to further God's gospel or to better your own life? When you can answer these, you will get to the root of your disappointments.

In Acts 8:18–25, the Bible shares a story of a sorcerer who wanted the power of God for all the wrong reasons:

> When Simon saw that the Spirit was given at the laying on of the apostles' hands, he offered them money and said, "Give me also this ability so that everyone on whom I lay my hands may receive the Holy Spirit."
>
> Peter answered: "May your money perish with you, because you thought you could buy the gift of God with money! You have no part or share in this ministry, because your heart is not right before God. Repent of this wickedness and pray to the Lord in the hope that he may forgive you for having such a thought in your heart. For I see that you are full of bitterness and captive to sin." (NIV)

We could want to become a Christian for many reasons: to feel connected to a good community, to please our family, to gain wealth and power. But the only reason we should have is to love God and to serve him. That is what God desires for us.

To learn how to have a heart of desire for God, read Psalm 27:4, which says,

> One thing I ask from the LORD, this only do I seek: that I may dwell in the house of the LORD all the

> days of my life, to gaze on the beauty of the LORD and to seek him in his temple. (NIV)

You need to turn to God and ask him for help. David, the writer of this psalm, was a man after God's own heart (1 Samuel 13:14), but even he couldn't become so through his own power. When we dwell in God's presence, we will receive a heart that longs for him more and more each day, and we will find satisfaction in our intimate communion with the Creator.

It's not about what we can offer or expect in return but about how we acknowledge God in a meaningful relationship. We find true fulfillment in knowing him deeply. Matthew 6:33 encourages believers to seek God's kingdom and his righteousness first: "Seek first his kingdom and his righteousness, and all these things will be given to you as well" (NIV). While blessings and expectations are not inherently wrong, a heart aligned with God's kingdom prioritizes his righteousness. Seeking his will precedes the pursuit of earthly desires.

May we all come before God with hearts that yearn for his presence, placing our trust in his timing and finding joy in seeking his will. As we nurture a relationship with God that transcends earthly pleasures, his heavenly blessings to us will flow. Our souls long for God, so take up your sword of prayer and turn to him. Through his power, you will arise, shine, and conquer.

Father, in the name of Jesus, I desire that you would be my greatest delight as I seek your beautiful face and find great joy in your presence. Lord, may you be my strength and help me to rise up for you. Amen.

Whether I am rich or poor, on a mountain or in a valley, you, Lord, are my heart's greatest desire.

Acknowledgments

I am profoundly grateful to God, whose unwavering love and guidance have been the cornerstone of this journey. Your faithfulness, favor, and provision have sustained me through every challenge and triumph. You are mine, and I am your beloved forever.

Thank you to my husband. Jesus displayed his love for me when he brought you into my life. You are my real-life Superman. I love you with all my heart.

To my sons, I hope I make you proud. Dream big and run with God.

Mommy, I wouldn't be here if it weren't for your prayers, encouragement, and support.

Misha, hands down, you are the best sister in the whole world. I love you so much.

Kim Crabill, your extravagant generosity has floored me. I am beyond grateful for your love, encouragement, prayer, and belief in me, all of which led me to this sweet moment. I am so thankful for you. I love you.

Last but certainly not least, to my whole family. Thank you for your endless support, encouragement, and understanding. Your love has been my anchor.

About the Author

Originally from Frankfort, Kentucky, Myshel Wilkins traveled with her missionary father and Ghanaian mother to various countries, speaking and leading worship from an early age.

Myshel graduated from Tennessee State University, where she earned a degree in political science. She was crowned Miss TSU and, in the same year, won the prestigious national title of Miss National Black Hall of Fame. She later earned a master's degree in organizational leadership from The Kings Seminary at The King's University in Southlake, Texas.

After moving to Nashville, Tennessee, and graduating from college, Myshel entered the Christian music arena, vocally supporting household names. She's toured with many artists, including Don Moen, Matthew West, TobyMac, and Mandisa. For several years, she has led Beth Moore's worship team for Moore's Living Proof Live events.

Opportunities later became available to Myshel to speak at retreats and conferences in addition to leading worship. Her mentor, Cece Winans, said, "It's a blessing